like the night

BOB DYLAN
and the road to the
Manchester Free Trade Hall

by C.P. Lee
with photographs by Paul Kelly

Helter Skelter
publishing

First published in 1998 by Helter Skelter Publishing,
4 Denmark Street, London WC2H 8LL

Reprinted 1998.

Designed by SAF Publishing
Cover photograph by Paul Kelly

A CIP record for this book is available from the British Library.

ISBN 1-900924-07-2

The publishers would like to thank the following for their help with this edition:
John Baldwin, Dave Hallbery, Mick Fish, Mike O'Connell and Greil Marcus.

Printed and bound in Great Britain by
Redwood Books, Trowbridge, Wiltshire

This book is dedicated to the memory of James Gabriel Lee
1915 - 1998

And to the loving joy of Pamela Lee - Onwards

CP Lee was 16 when he went to see Bob Dylan and The Hawks at the Free Trade Hall. He was so overwhelmed that he went on to become founder member of 70's rock iconoclasts Alberto Y Lost Trios Paranoias. He became an unlikely academic in the late 80's, gaining a Doctorate in popular music, and now teaches cultural studies in the Department of Media and Performance at the University of Salford.

Paul Kelly was 15 when he took the photographs of Bob Dylan and The Hawks at the Free Trade Hall. He was so overwhelmed that he went on to become a psychiatric social worker. He retired in the 1990's and went on to become unwittingly embroiled in the production of this book.

Contents

FOREWORD

In 1971 I got hold of a bootleg recording that I'd read about in the underground press. It was called *Bob Dylan - Live At The Albert Hall*. I rushed home with it, eager and excited to hear a performance that was already being described as legendary. When I put it on my record player I found I was in for quite a shock, emotionally, spiritually and almost physically.

The level of commitment and playing by Dylan and The Band was everything that I'd expected. I'd been present for one of the gigs that early spring of 1966 and had dreamed, wished and hoped that a live recording would come out one day. Now, here it was, a document of a period of intense creativity tinged with madness, and the mindless barracking of an audience who felt that Dylan had somehow 'betrayed' them.

But as I sat and listened to the album there came a growing sense of familiarity. It wasn't that the numbers were the same as those he had played at the Free Trade Hall, it was more to do with the audience interaction. A friend who shared my flat at the time, Bob Harding, said, 'This isn't the Albert Hall, this is Manchester.' Like crazy archaeologists we played and replayed the cuts, reconstructing the events of the evening as we went along. Digging deeper and deeper into the weirdness of that May evening. Yes, that was when the slow hand-clapping started. Yes, that was when the woman went up to Dylan with the note and the audience had applauded. Yes, that was when the guy had shouted 'Judas!' - just before 'Like A Rolling Stone'.

And so, despite the perceived wisdom of the time and the prevailing attitudes in the music press, I always figured it was Manchester.

Cut to 1978/9, and for some reason lost in the mists of time, I'd written a letter about the gig to a local magazine, *The New Manchester Review*. Within a week I'd received a couple of phone calls and eventually somebody came round to my house and interviewed me for a Dylan fanzine. I had no other evidence than my own recollections, but I could argue the case with a passion. I thought, 'what the heck?' and then I thought no more about it.

Until, that is 1991, when I registered to do a PhD at the Manchester Institute of Popular Culture. My Doctoral thesis was going to be on the history of Popular Music in Manchester and I felt it was essential to include Dylan's 1966 Free Trade Hall gig as one of the pivotal points in the formation of the 'scene'. If I was to include it, I needed solid evidence to back up my argument about the origins of the recording. And so a quest began to track down information as regards the world tour and that one night in particular. I didn't reach 'write up' stage until 1995 and that's when I put a request out over the Internet for any information regarding the mysterious bootleg recording. One respondent, Ben Taylor, downloaded information for me off the Highway 61 mailing list plus other relevant pages from the archives of Rec Music.Dylan, the Bob Dylan Newsgroup. (See Appendix)

The material consisted of a series of ongoing debates taking place in cyberspace about the origins of the recording. What we knew for sure was that they were of a very high standard, professionally made, and that they might, at one point, have been scheduled for release by Dylan's record company Sony/Columbia. But where exactly the recording had been made was still being hotly contested. When it came it came to one of the primary reasons for considering Manchester I was quite surprised to see my name mentioned along with the assertion that 'CP Lee has always said it was made in Manchester.'!

So there I was, in the rather peculiar position of finding myself as the primary source for my own rumour!

Bit by bit though, the evidence piled up. A letter from *The Oldham Chronicle* here, a *Times* review there, until finally the case seemed closed and I wrote the chapter. Then fate intervened in the shape of a digitally re-mastered CD entitled *Guitars Kissing & The Contemporary Fix*. This was the complete Manchester concert and was billed as such. Finally the perceived wisdom regarding the event came down on my side and the recording was officially acknowledged as the Free Trade Hall. The origins of *GK&TCF* (as it came to be known in Dylan circles) as a commercial product are, as with all things bootleg, impossible to pin down, but the story goes that it was made up as a test copy for consideration as a legitimate release and when it was shelved a disgruntled employee decided to take the (out)law into their own hands and spread it around.

Being a digital recording the quality is quite superb and the CD has gone on to become one of the most popular unofficial Bob Dylan recordings available. The reviews that it has garnered from a wide variety of sources match, if not indeed, overtake those awarded to the original vinyl release. Words such as 'Stunning,' 'Brilliant,' and 'Jaw dropping' have been freely bandied about.

Fate intervened again in the shape of Bleddyn Butcher who had been asked to write a short piece on the concert for *Mojo* Magazine. He interviewed me and spurred on by the interest shown in Bleddyn's article I delved even deeper into the events of that night.

Anyway, as a result of my researches I got thinking that the chapter deserved a full size book all to itself. Then an old friend, Steve Currie, who was also there that night, told me of another friend of his who'd taken photographs of the concert. A quick phone call and a meeting in a city centre pub resulted in my joining forces with Paul Kelly, who at the age of fifteen took the photos you'll find in this book.

Andy Spinoza, from *The Manchester Evening News*, published an article about our search for survivors - those who were there that night. A flurry of phone calls and letters were received, and resulted in a series of interviews with a wide variety of people who'd been present at the gig thirty years before. A surprisingly large number of people had kept memorabilia as well as their memories intact, and soon we had a pool of information to draw on. Interviews took place in people's living rooms, pubs and work places. Everybody who contacted us had a story to tell and gradually we were able to piece together a coherent view of the events.

So why is the Free Trade Hall recording so important?

Because it is amongst the clearest evidence that we have of the battle being waged by Dylan in his efforts to tread a new path - following the almost apocalyptic vision that seemed to have gripped him at the time. And, more precisely, the opposition that Dylan got from many members of his audience. To imagine a popular artist today being called 'Judas' in the middle of a concert is unthinkable. To Dylan in 1966 it was an everyday occurrence.

Around early 1965, Bob Dylan had embarked on a musical odyssey that would place him in direct opposition to a large proportion of his fan base. He made a conscious decision to extend and go beyond the confines of 'Folk', whatever that was. Slowly, but surely, over the next eighteen months he steered himself in a direction that no other contemporary performer had ever gone in before, and the results of his creativity can be heard in his recorded output from that period, all the way from *Bringing It All Back Home* to *Blonde On Blonde*.

By 1966 Dylan was not only at the peak of his creativity but also of his fame. Dozens of other artists were rushing to record his songs, interviews were sought, his every word and utterance hung on. His face graced the front pages not just of Pop magazines, but other, more august journals such as the *Saturday Evening Post*, *The New York Times* and *Time Magazine*. Dylan was a cultural phenomenon, rapidly in danger of becoming a messiah.

Dylan's life in the two years leading up to the start of 1966 had seen increasing pressures placed on him. By the time the world tour proper began in February, these pressures would become crushing. That the vastly increased workload took its toll physically and mentally has never been denied. Dylan resorted to a kind of alchemical pharmacy in order to carry on, but that which was designed to give him an edge almost pushed him over it.

Ironically the motorbike crash that nearly killed him on July 29th 1966, probably saved his life. Dylan could finally stop and take stock of his life, be with his family and rest up. This is exactly what he did. He also adopted the mantle of a recluse and holed up in Woodstock. For nearly eighteen months Dylan's fans waited for a sign, for anything that would give us a clue as to what was going on.

It finally came in the form of a new album called *John Wesley Harding*, and it was as big a surprise as any of his others that had come before. He had gone back to an acoustic style that couldn't have been more dramatically different than its electric predecessors. But that's another story. This book is the story of Bob Dylan, his world tour and one night in Manchester in 1966.

CHAPTER ONE
First Time Around

It's a fairly quiet Tuesday in May 1964 as Bob Dylan and his manager Albert Grossman speed through the streets of Manchester, southwards towards the studios of ATV television. Coming from the Midland Hotel in town they go along the drab arterial Wilmslow Road, past the main University campus towards Rusholme. The name J F Blood Antiques excites their curiosity for a moment, as does the Temperance Bar, a pub which serves only Dandelion and Burdock and Ginger Beer. Next they see the L'Auberge De France restaurant, one of the few concessions towards a kind of cosmopolitan modernity. They're digging the oddly positioned Italian Consulate above a delicatessen near Dickinson Road, but then drift into boredom mode along the south bound route out of Manchester with its big bus depot on the side of Owen's Park hiding from the sight of a terraced football ground that was once host to the UK Cup Final in 1893 (Wolves versus Everton. Wolves won 1-0). If it's in their consciousness at all it seems like a kind of Post-World War Two England mixed with New Jersey at its worst. Alert again, they hit Withington Village, little changed from the century before, still boasting a firestation, an ancient milestone, and a horse trough. After that bit of questionable quaintness they're back on a seemingly interminable ride from Post Victorian ghetto to the outer suburban whimsy of semi-detacheds which connect Withington with Didsbury.

Dylan and Grossman comment on the irony of the claim in the previous night's *Manchester Evening News* that where they are bound is a 'leafy, tree lined suburb', though in essence that's what Didsbury is, and much more beside.

By the turn of the century Didsbury had become a place for artistic and liberal refugees fleeing the overcrowding of the inner city area, be it of England or Europe. Members of the Halle Orchestra now live there, with lawyers, professors and filmmakers, such as Paul Rotha, one of the founders of the English documentary school, and writer of seminal works on Eisenstein and Krackauer. Media megastars, like leader writers from the *Manchester Guardian*, have followed the legendary C P Scott and taken advantage of the village-like atmosphere which seems to them to set it aside from the smoke driven, industrial hodge podge that makes up the major urban conurbation of Greater Manchester. For the residents, in a weird way, Didsbury is a place apart, a place to unwind, where you can stroll along the lanes by Stenner Farm, check out the cows, attend the Didsbury Show and see the resident poacher with his fox on a lead, and take a drink in any of the many pubs that dot its main roads and byways. Love it or loathe it, Didsbury is the countryside in the middle of a city.

In terms of England in the early 1960s, Didsbury has led the way, with its writers and artists, academics and journos, while being perfect simulacra of a by-gone age. If you want, you can get your washing done by the huge laundry on the side of Didsbury Park. The Co-op on Wilmslow Road prides itself on the service it offers, like downstairs there's a grocery store (orders delivered by young boys on bikes), and upstairs you find a gentlemen's outfitters complete with full length mirrors that, if positioned correctly, give you a display of yourself into infinity, and counters full of 'sleeve garters' and 'Attaboy' gentlemen's hats mixed in with collar studs and cufflinks. Silk dressing gowns jostle for position with displays of 'New! Man-made polyester pyjamas!'

But now there's something new on the horizon in Didsbury. Something that arrived there in the mid 1950s - television.

Dylan and Grossman's taxi arrives at the studio on schedule, where they are greeted by one very excited young man called Neville. Neville has one of those jobs you dream of but you don't know how to find. His responsi-

bility is looking after the artistes who appear on the shows produced in the Didsbury studio, a kind of hospitality go-fer. More and more people turning up at the Capitol Building are radically out of the ordinary, much more interesting than the run-of-the mill music hall entertainers, comics and singers hoping to graduate to some sort of national stardom through the exposure they get on this new medium. He'd just done the go-fering for the Rolling Stones who had appeared on a Variety show alongside a performing lion (they shared the same Bed and Breakfast too on Moreland

Road, but with the lion in a cage outside). More of the emerging Rock Hipocracy are trekking to the studios to appear on this or that, but here any minute now is somebody that Neville is unbelievably excited by.

He'd first heard of Dylan about a year before when a friend had sat him down and made him listen to Dylan's first album. Neville was already initiated into folk blues. Mancunian youth had been obsessed by Black American music for nearly a decade and this album by a young white American soaked in folk blues makes perfect sense to Neville. He and his mates have bought albums by white, folk blues players Ric Von Schmidt and Dave Van Ronk and all sorts of other weirdness that has recently emerged out of Greenwich Village and elsewhere, but here is a guy whose music really makes it. For Neville, Dylan is a revelation and an epiphany. God he's excited.

School Lane is quiet on the morning of the 14th of May. The traffic is light along the road. It isn't Saturday so there aren't any fans on the steps of the Capitol Building hoping to get autographs. Today the only person anxiously waiting for the two Americans is Neville, who can't believe his luck. He's thinking like there can be no bigger fan of the man he is waiting for, and he hadn't even known that Dylan was booked in until he read the call sheets when he arrived at work that morning. And now, in a way, it was going to be like meeting James Dean and The Beatles all rolled into one - only even better.

Grossman gets out of the cab first and pays off the driver. Dressed in a grey suit and with his hair just beginning to grow longer than conventional length, the slightly chubby New Yorker looks like a grumpy version of Ben Franklin. He's followed out of the cab by Dylan, carrying a guitar case and clutching a holdall to himself like a safety vest. Dylan doesn't look like Neville imagines he would. Gone are the Guthriesque work-clothes and little black cap that he'd been wearing in all the publicity pictures printed in the English press and shown on album covers. Dylan's hair is a lot longer now, wilder, kind of like a greaser's but less tailored. Black shades match a black jacket over a denim tab-collared shirt. Blue jeans and cowboy boots complete the ensemble. Neville is surprised at how painfully thin and small Dylan looks. Like a waif, unprotected and lost. Dylan and Grossman stare across the road away from the TV studio, at a pub called The Parrs Wood Hotel. It's closed.

Neville sprints down the steps to greet them and explains who he is.

Disconcertingly, Grossman peers through his glasses and grunts. Dylan says nothing. Neville leads them up the stairs and through reception into the maze of corridors that will take them to their dressing room. When they get to Dressing Room B in the basement Neville shows them in and asks if they'd like tea.

'Tea?' replies Grossman peering over the tops of his glasses.

'Or coffee?' Neville says, remembering they're Americans.

'No thank you. We'll be fine,' Grossman answer in his polite yet slightly dismissive tone. Dylan says nothing but stares blankly around the room.

'I'll leave you to it then', says Neville, slightly flustered. 'If you need anything, just call me.'

As he's about to go out of the dressing room door Neville turns and speaks directly to Dylan, 'I really like your music man.' For the first time, Dylan looks up at him and smiles.

Throughout the rest of the morning and lunch, Dylan and Grossman don't stir from their dressing room. Coffee and sandwiches are called for and Sydney Carter and his director pop down for a chat, but Neville doesn't see any more of them until he goes down to tell them that it's time for the run-through.

'No it's not.' Grossman tells him firmly. 'Bob doesn't need to do a run-through. It's just him and his guitar. They know the songs.'

'But they don't,' says Neville earnestly, 'It's not on the schedule. It's not down on the shooting script.' Neville proffers the clipboard with its running order on it for Grossman to peruse. He ignores it and stares hard at Neville.

'Bob doesn't need to do a rehearsal... Do you Bob?'

'No way man,' Dylan replies from the dressing room couch.

Neville can dig this. He's fully aware of Dylan and Dylan's importance and to a degree Neville can sympathise with anybody who wants to avoid the endless set-ups and run-throughs that TV demands, so he decides to go and explain to the director himself.

After a furious discussion Neville somehow pulls it off. He manages to persuade the Hallelujah production crew that the only thing they need is a two-cam set up after Sydney Carter's introduction. Bob is to play two songs and that will be it. They agree and send Neville back downstairs to say okay to Grossman.

Back in the basement, Neville knocks tentatively at the door and enters the dressing room.

'So you dig what I do?' Dylan asks Neville.

'Yeah man. I've been listening to you for ages.'

'You guys know what's happening in America?' queries Dylan peering over his glasses.

Neville can't quite understand what Dylan means. Civil rights? The Kennedy assassination? Surf music?

'You know? The kind of music we're playing and everything?' continues Dylan.

Neville understands and reels off a list of the blues and folk players that he's got albums by.

'No man, I mean, who do you really like?'

Neville nervously repeats the list of names, Bukka White, Muddy Waters, Broonzy, Big Joe Turner, Woodie Guthrie, Cisco Houston..... And of course Dylan...

Dylan seems satisfied.

'OK. What would you like me to play on the show?' Dylan asks, picking up his guitar.

Neville can't believe it. Dylan is asking him what he'd like to hear? This is almost too much. He runs through all the Dylan stuff he can recall in his blown-out head. A memory stirs. 'How about Baby Let Me Follow You Down?' Neville asks.

Dylan makes an effort to play the Ric Von Schmidt tune. First it's in 'G', then he tries 'E'. Dylan struggles but can't find the descending 'D' shape from seventh fret. Eventually he gives up.

'I'm sorry man, I just can't remember it,' Dylan says, looking up from his guitar, as if baffled. Grossman shuffles through papers he's taken out of his briefcase. They all stare at the uneaten sandwiches.

'I know man! Off *Freewheeling.* 'Don't Think Twice It's Alright'. Neville calls excitedly.

Dylan starts strumming the chords, 'That's cool Neville. Yeah, I know that one. And I tell you what... I'll do a new one for you too.'

Neville can hardly answer. He's staring at Dylan's right hand. As Bob fits an harmonica into the holder that's round his shoulders Neville can't help but notice how nicotine stained are the fingers that are grappling with the Hohner Marine Band harp. Dylan's fingernail on his index finger is cracked and blackened. In point of fact, the whole dressing room is muggy with cigarette smoke. Both Grossman and Dylan have been chain-smoking the whole time they've been there and the ashtrays are full of Marlboro butts. Grossman though blows Neville's mind because he's never seen anybody smoke cigarettes through their fist before and he watches in fascination as Grossman lights up another Marlboro.

'Neville?' Grossman exhales, leaning over towards him and peering into his face, 'Do you think I could ask you a favour?'

'Of course man,' replies Neville only too eager to help out his two new friends.

'Bob and I need to be on our own for a few minutes. Do you think you could go outside and mind the door?' Grossman asks politely.

'Yeah, sure man.' Neville replies.

'And no one. Repeat, no one is to come in Neville. Do you understand?' Grossman quizzes Neville.

Neville smiles at Dylan who nods back at him as Neville closes the door. His last glimpse is of Dylan walking towards Grossman who is reaching into his briefcase.

Ten minutes later the director calls down to Neville that the studio is ready for the young American singer, so he boldly raps on the door and announces himself.

Grossman opens the door and lets Neville in. Dylan is coming out of the toilet. Grossman smiles enigmatically as he ushers Neville through the door.

'Bob's ready now.' says Grossman.

Neville looks at Dylan and can't quite believe his eyes. Dylan is actually stumbling towards his guitar. After a brief struggle he manages to get the

strap over his head and then begins the monumental struggle to put on his harmonica holder. Neville knows that they are ready on the studio floor but also knows that there is no way that he can rush Dylan or even get across to him the sense of urgency that is in the air. Dylan is his own master now.

Dylan wriggles and twists. Eventually the harmonica holder is in place and he stands triumphantly, if uncertainly, in front of Neville.

'Let's go man', Dylan tells Neville.

Grossman nods in affirmation.

So off they set, the sorry trio, down onto the studio floor where the assembled cast and crew of 'Hallelujah' are assembled awaiting their American 'friend', the wunderkind of 'protest', the one and only Bob Dylan, the young man whose song 'The Times They Are A Changing' is hitting the charts in the USA and beginning to make a dent in the UK. He is the hottest thing in the folk world, like, ever, and Bob has a few surprises up his sleeve for the producers.

First though, is the major problem of getting Dylan onto his stool. The director has laid on a tasteful backdrop and the opening shot is a segue away from Sidney Carter to a secondary shot of Bob. After the intro the spare camera has to dolly across the studio and fill in the unrehearsed blanks. If Dylan remains seated in one spot this isn't going to present too much trouble for the director up in the gallery. Grossman decides to stay on the studio floor out of camera shot and Neville has to help Bob onto the stool.

Dylan is settled now and a flustered Carter begins his intro....

'And now "Hallelujah" is proud to present to you a new, young voice from the American folk scene. A young man who is being hailed as the natural successor to Woodie Guthrie. A young man whose songs such as "Blowin' In The Wind" and "The Times They Are A-Changin" speak not only to his generation but to all of us - Bob Dylan.'

To the amazement of all but Neville, Dylan blasts off with a smouldering version of 'Don't Think Twice It's Alright', from his second album *Freewheeling*. This time there's no delicate fingerpicking. The strings are flatpicked in an Okie hard cut, solid, driven, like a woodsman with a particularly stubborn tree. But the central sound that emerges from a tune that's a goodbye as well as an hosanna is the strident, thrusting of the harmonica playing. Four times the lyrics are punctuated by the reedy trill of the Hohner Marine Band blasting out its independence. The pace of the tune is fast, the words laid down as a firmly placed statement of circumstance rather than as a prevarication. Dylan means business and he's taking no prisoners. 'Don't Think Twice', here in Didsbury, is, to paraphrase Lord Buckley, 'solid sent, crashed out, in the silk, fifteen foot down with a concrete wig!'

It ends almost as suddenly as it has begun and Dylan coughs a couple of times. Then he speaks, and it seems to Neville that Dylan's speaking to him.

'That was a love song....'

Dylan fumbles around for an harmonica in a different key. As he puts it into the holder he carries on speaking....

'This is an hallucination... atery song...'

Dylan then throws the studio into confusion. It's a brand new song. A song that goes beyond the bounds of their practised credulity. This is like no Dylan song the producer, the director, the researcher, Sidney Carter or even Neville has ever heard Dylan play before. It's a song that a religious programme like 'Hallelujah', liberal though its remit is, would never be able to comprehend. It is 'Chimes of Freedom'.

Dylan began writing it in February during a trans-American car trip which took him on an odyssey that encompassed the rapidly evolving phantasmagoria of the evolutionary underground in the States. It's a song that marks a kind of transition point in his consciousness and capabilities as a tunesmith. 'Chimes Of Freedom' transcends 'protest' and enters the realms of poetic beatification. It is a benediction and it's a curse. Dylan does not lie when he introduces it as 'an hallucination - atery song'. 'Chimes' is the transition point between Dylan the cocksure young jackal yapping at the heels of the olde garde lions, and Dylan the spokesperson of a generation, a singer capable of articulating thoughts that haven't yet entered our heads. It's a song that firmly places Dylan at the forefront of contemporary songwriting and maybe even, social commentary. The studio is stunned.

Dylan finishes, looks around a little bemused and then slides gently off his stool. Neville grabs him and holds him up. Grossman looks on and smiles. Dylan looks up at Neville.

'Not bad, eh?' Dylan grins.

'Not bad man,' replies Neville, helping Dylan stand up.

'Could we have quiet in the studio please while we check the tape?' the floor manager calls out. After a few seconds have gone by he comes over to Dylan and Neville. 'The director isn't quite sure about the take. Sorry to trouble you Bob, but would you mind awfully doing it again, just to be on the safe side?' he asks.

'Yes he would mind! - Very much!' storms Grossman joining Dylan and Neville by the stool. 'Bob is very tired and if you assholes can't get your shots right then that's not his problem!'

Grossman plucks Dylan from Neville's arms and stalks out of the studio with him. The director comes down from the gallery and pleads with Neville to see what he can do. Neville just shrugs.

After consultations with the technical crew, the director and producer decide to go along with Grossman and Neville is despatched to the dressing room to tell the two Americans that they can go. This Neville duly proceeds to do.

As he enters Dressing Room B, Grossman is stomping up and down the floor while Dylan is laying down on the couch looking, how shall we say, relaxed.

'I want to really thank you man, that was great,' says Neville.

'Can we go now?' shouts Grossman, staring intently at Neville.

'Did you like it man?' Dylan says quietly, halting Grossman momentarily.

'Yeah man. It was really great,' replies Neville, meaning every word.

'There you go man,' says Dylan to Grossman, 'I told you they'd like it.'

'Sure Bob, sure.' Grossman grunts, grabbing his briefcase. 'Can you call us a cab?'

'Cab?' says Neville.

'A taxi', snorts Grossman.

'No problem,' replies Neville. Leading the way out of the dressing room, Grossman goes first, Dylan picks himself up and shuffles along behind him.

At reception as they are waiting for their taxi back to the Midland Hotel, Dylan relapses into silence as Grossman looks up and down at Neville.

'Erm, Bob wants you to have this.' Grossman says handing Neville an LP in a plain sleeve.

'What is it?'

'It's a copy of Bob's new album,' replies Grossman.

Neville can't believe it. Albert Grossman has just handed him a white-label copy of *The Times They Are A Changing*. He's still looking at it as their taxi pulls up outside the Capitol Building. As Dylan and Grossman career towards it, Dylan turns to Neville and takes him by the hand. Neville can't believe how small and cold Dylan's hand is. Limp and waxy.

'Thanks for everything man,' Dylan drawls, eyes half-shut.

'Thank you man. I'll see you next time you're in Manchester.'

Dylan would return to Manchester, but the next two times would be under very different circumstances.

CHAPTER TWO
It Could Even Be Like A Myth

It's time now to put Dylan within the context of the 'Folk Scene' and Popular Music as it stood in the 1960s. We have to do this in order to be able to understand why the world tour aroused such animosity in so many people, and, at Manchester in particular, why this led to the outburst of pent-up ferocity that culminated in the 'Judas!' shout.

The people who booed, slow hand-clapped, heckled, whistled and walked out belonged to a fraternity, an almost semi-mystical coalition of like-minded purists who referred to themselves as 'Folk Fans'. That is, followers of what was spoken of at the time as 'The Folk Revival', and who I shall refer to as the 'Traditionalists'.

Why Abandon Safety?

The Revival in England (which was more or less paralleled in America, as we shall see later) had started in the early 1950s when young music fans had extended their listening away from Tin Pan Alley Pop. They were looking for something different from the mainstream and it came to them in the form of Jazz.

Later in this chapter, I try to identify why people choose to go against the mainstream of popular entertainment forms. Why abandon the safety of the BBC's Northern Dance Orchestra playing a selection of Tin Pan Alley hits in favour of tracking down obscure cuts by Louis Armstrong or

King Oliver? There is an air of perversity about such deliberate reactions to the norm, a missionary zeal and a whiff of the trainspotter. A delight in being different. Singled out. There is also an almost spiritual emotion attached to it; bonding, being brought together by a clandestine musical taste, the participation in transcendental ritual, the shared thrill of an illicit love, the exclusivity of a superior knowledge.

But jazz too had its cliques, its schisms, its heretics, its martyrs and its saints. Far from being straightforward jazz was split into two camps - Traditionalists and Modernists. The form which fed into the Folk Revival was Traditional, or 'Trad,' and this is the one we'll look at briefly. There was an element of purity about the form the music took. An important word at the time, one which was to take on even greater significance in the 1960s was 'commerciality', or rather, the lack of it. It was believed that somehow this traditional music was 'cleaner', less tainted than the maudlin love songs pouring out of Radio Luxembourg. The music was more 'authentic' for coming from a Black American tradition. While Swing shared the same roots, it was viewed as having been taken over and sanitized by Whites. Trad jazz by contrast, was still unsullied by modern commercial forces. Also, there was an air of deviancy about liking tracks that had emerged from Basin Street forty/fifty years before. A hint of the forbidden -.of the underworld, and the glamour of the unknown.

The audience for Trad were known as 'Ravers' and deliberately dressed down. They adopted a kind of unique British middle class concept of Bohemianism. In his book *Owning Up* George Melly remembered it:

'.... an extreme sloppiness was de rigeur, both on stage and off. The duffle coat was a cult object, sandals with socks a popular if repulsive fad, beards common and bits of battle dress, often dyed navy-blue, almost a uniform.'

Ban The Bomb, CND and 'Jazz On A Summer's Day', the first of the Windsor festivals (which later metamorphosed into the Windsor Jazz & Blues, then finally - Rock Festival), Trad was mainly a student pursuit, a middle class thing. But out of Trad came a person who, along with the influence of Elvis Presley, was to revolutionise English youth and English music. That person was Lonnie Donegan.

Putting On The Agony - Putting On The Style

Donegan came from a musical family based in the north of England. His father was a violinist in the National Scottish Orchestra and Donegan too had become a professional musician. After moving to London in the early 1950s he became a guitarist/singer in the Crane River Jazz Band with Rich Collyer until settling down into the highly influential Chris Barber Band. Barber was the purist's prime mover and in the typical fashion of puritanical fervour adopted by the Trad revivalists became an ardent (and noted) musicologist in the quest for truth. Both he and Donegan discovered Jazz's contemporary and partial progenitor, Blues. Barber's proselytizing meant that with his success as a Trad performer he could invite Blues musicians such as Muddy Waters to appear in concert with him on stage in England throughout the late 1950s. In fact they played the Free Trade Hall together in 1958.

Donegan too had become a Blues enthusiast and as early as 1953 was given a featured spot in the Crane River Band, playing his version of an American street corner Folk Blues style known as 'Skiffle'. This proved so popular that he carried on performing his feature spot when he moved to the Chris Barber Band. Donegan's version of Skiffle was a kind of anglicised Folk Blues played on guitar, backed by a bass and with a rhythm provided either by drums, or the simple expedient of thimble covered fingers strummed across an old fashioned metal wash board. The old-style train and work songs became a staple of Skiffle thanks to their light, fast pacing, and it was a live recording by the Barber Band made at The Royal Festival Hall in 1955 that unleashed the Skiffle boom on an unsuspecting world.

Donegan's section received repeated plays on the BBC Light Programme and eventually a single, 'Rock Island Line', written by Black Folk Blues player Huddie Leadbetter, better known as Leadbelly, was released as a single on the Decca label in late 1955. By the end of 1956 it had sold over a million copies worldwide.

Donegan's influence was twofold. Firstly, he inspired thousands of youngsters across England to start playing; there can hardly be a member of the first wave of English Beat groups who hadn't played in a Skiffle group (The Quarrymen, The Beatles' first incarnation started out playing

skiffle). Secondly, he led a lot of young people on a search for the origi-
nals that he based his repertoire on, and through that they had discovered
Lonnie Johnson, writer of 'Diggin' My Potatoes' and Big Bill Broonzy.
That in turn had led them to white artists such as Woodie Guthrie, Cisco
Houston, et al.

From Such Humble Beginnings

What we have then is a significant group of youngsters who found their
way into Folk Blues via Skiffle. These adherents are amongst the first
wave of the revival. Before dealing with what I might term the second
wave, that is, people like me who got into it in the early 1960s, we need to
look at the extant English Folk scene as it stood at the time, and more importantly, how it developed into the movement that would launch attacks
on Dylan when he went electric.

In the 1950s there was a second group of music fans who were more
oriented to the indigenous music of the British Isles and ethnic music in
general. This was a position that had been nurtured from the beginning of
the 20th Century when an organisation called The English Folk Dance and
Song Society had been founded. The EFDS was located at Cecil Sharp
House in London, and it's still there. Founding members Cecil Sharp and
the Reverend Baring Gould were two of the principal collectors of native
songs in England, travelling around the countryside on bicycles, armed
with cylinder recorders to try and preserve the rich oral tradition that they
saw as rapidly disappearing. Sharp also travelled to the Appalachian
Mountains in the United States to observe and chronicle the transition of
popular ballads from the old country to the new. While there he met John
Lomax, who with the help of his son Alan, was starting to record American folk music on the first actual portable recording disc player. The two
exchanged ideas and recordings and Sharp's influence enthused John
Lomax sufficiently to persuade the prestigious Smithsonian Institute to
fund his travels across America documenting different aspects of Folk
music. It was his son however, who would become the more famous in
this area of scholarship.

As a result of their research the Lomaxes, father and son, were able to
bring to public attention many of the musicians who would become main-

stays of the Folk Blues revival of the 1950s and 60s. For instance, in 1941 he stopped by Stovell's Plantation in Mississippi and recorded a young man by the name of McKinley Morganfield. A year later when he returned McKinley had changed his name to Muddy Waters and had decided to move to Chicago where he could find enough work to become a professional musician. He did and became one of the leading lights in what was later to become known as 'urban', or Chicago R'n'B. It's not unreasonable to speculate that without Lomax's intervention the young Morganfield may never have felt inspired to make the move and we would have been denied one of the most important influences on Popular Music that America has given to the world. For instance, The Rolling Stones would have had to have chosen another name, having taken theirs from a Muddy Waters' song. Might it have made a difference also to 'Like A Rolling Stone?'

Alan Lomax, as we shall see, was also later to have a profound effect upon the English Folk Revival.

The younger generation of Folk fans who began to emerge in the late 1950s and early 1960s were influenced by a dissatisfaction with the overall banality of the Pop scene, with its endless retreads of tried and tested formulas, its insipid cover versions of American chart hits and its crass commerciality. The escape route from the vapidity that many saw Pop becoming was to be found in the emergence of the Folk club. Like their counterparts in the Beat clubs, a high percentage of the Folk venues were to be found in the coffee bars of major cities. It wasn't uncommon for some venues to hedge their bets and put on both types of music on alternate nights.

Bert Lloyd & Ewan MacColl

There was still, in some parts of the country, a rich, vibrant oral Folk tradition that TV and radio hadn't eradicated. There are quite a few factors in the revivalist atmosphere of the 1950s and 60s that predate the denim-capped and Dylanesque flavour of the renaissance of Folk. Perhaps the most important of these has to be the A.L. Lloyd-inspired maintenance of the English Folk tradition throughout the 1940s and 50s. A scion of the Communist Party of Great Britain, Bert Lloyd wielded great influence on the extant Folk scene of that period, organising festivals, holding song-writing competitions and generally encouraging working class people in following what he perceived of as their traditional values. Lloyd, along with many others of his time and before him, had a penchant for mediating songs that they collected. That is to say, the song they had gathered could legitimately be 'amended' if it failed to fit their bill of 'political correctness', or needed musically 'correcting'.

One of the greatest songs to have emerged from the entrenched CPGB (Communist Party of Great Britain) ramparts in the immediate post-war period is Ewan MacColl's 'Dirty Old Town'. MacColl typifies all that was good and all that was bad about the Folk Revival, and it's no surprise that he worked hand in glove with Bert Lloyd to bring about the English renaissance along party lines.

MacColl was born James Miller in Salford (the place setting for 'Dirty Old Town' - not Dublin as a lot of younger people now seem to think!) into a staunchly left wing working class family. Young James was brought up in the grim, twilight world of the Great Depression made (in)famous by Walter Greenwood's classic novel of life in the Salford of that period, *Love On The Dole*. The 1930s saw the last gasp of the era of working class intellectualism in Salford, and over at the Workers' Arts Club in Weaste, soon to become immortalised as 'The croft' in 'Dirty Old Town,' the young songwriter was inspired to form a radical street theatre group which did Agit-Prop style performances outside factory gates and radical meeting places. They were called The Red Megaphones, named after a Russian Constructivist theatre group. It was for them that he wrote the first of many classic songs, 'The Manchester Rambler.'

During the Second World War James Miller changed his name to Ewan MacColl. Why has always been a cloudy issue. His critics maintain that it was in order to avoid conscription; others, that it was in tribute to, or emulation of, Scottish singer Hamish Imlach. His widow, Peggy Seeger, sister of American Folk legend Pete Seeger and mother of Pop singer Kirsty MacColl, refuses to join in the debate.

Ewan MacColl's influence on the English Folk Revival of the 1950s and onwards came about as a result of meeting Alan Lomax just after the end of the Second World War. Inspired by his father John's work documenting American folk songs, Alan was now in England recording the remnants of the oral tradition here. He put MacColl in touch with Bert Lloyd and in 1951 the three of them began working on a radio series for the BBC entitled 'Ballads And Blues'. This was a revolutionary fusion of musical styles, encompassing British Trad Jazz, alongside the likes of Big Bill Broonzy and West Indian Calypso singer, Fitzroy Coleman. Programmes were recorded at venues like the Theatre Workshop in Stratford East, and The Princess Louise pub in High Holborn. Audience participation was directly encouraged and the dialectical theories of the Folk Revival were much discussed.

Too Much Uncle Sam

All this discussion came about as the result of the publication in 1951, by the National Cultural Committee of the CPGB, of a pamphlet entitled The *American Threat To British Culture*. It opened with a critique of what the authors called 'American Big Business', which they claimed was a shadowy institution that lay behind the dynamics of American Mass/Popular Culture. A culture, they asserted, that was designed to brainwash the ordinary mass of people into 'dollar worship', racism, brutality and 'gangsterism'. It claimed this was being done through the mediums of books, comics, films and Popular Music. It claimed this was a plot. It claimed this was nothing less than cultural imperialism. In terms of the problem facing English contemporary music it stated -

'The plight of British songwriters is so desperate that the Song Writers Guild of Great Britain have made a formal protest to the BBC against the anti-British attitude of so many performers and dance bands. Out of twenty of the most popular current songs, seventeen are American, one is French and two are British.... British singers repeat the identical US settings parrot-wise. British crooners ape the Americans in slurred vowels and forced inflexions.'

CPGB, 1951

The committee also noted problems with 'our own folk songs and dances'. This was despite the sterling work being undertaken by comrade A.L. Lloyd and the Worker's Music Association. Significantly, the committee found that the 'proletariat' appeared to prefer 'Popular' music rather than indigenous British Folk music. The conclusion that the authors drew from this was that the People would have to be 'educated into their own culture' and this process of 'education' was to be carried out by re-invigorating the native Folk tradition, and preserving it from 'contamination' by American influences.

Thus galvanised by Party dictates, MacColl and Lloyd kick-started the revival into life by opening firstly, the Blues and Ballad Club in London in 1953, and then, not long after, the highly influential Singers Clubs. In 1957 MacColl claimed that there were 1,500 Singers Clubs around Britain with an 11,000 strong membership. Although this might be termed a success in terms of building up a musical movement virtually from scratch, the rigid Communist Party line in dialectics concerning the style and content of what could and what could not be sung in the clubs was not only ludicrous, but was to have tragic ramifications for the British Folk scene for years to come.

What Ewan MacColl espoused was a perverted form of what was then known as 'nationalism' and would now be termed 'political correctness'. And yet, the experiment had started so boldly. MacColl told Robin Denselow in Denselow's book *When The Music's Over*,

'When Alan Lomax came along with this music that had proved popular with generations and generations, I thought, "This is what we should be exploring!"'

In the early days of the revival MacColl had found no difficulty in jumping onstage with Ken Collyer's Jazzmen and singing a Black Alabama prison song with them, but within a couple of years the traditional British left wing distrust of anything American had overcome his musical instincts. For MacColl, along with so many others, even, ironically, from the Right, America equated with the Great Satan - Capitalism.

Again he told Denselow -

'I became concerned that we had a whole generation who were becoming quasi-Americans, and I felt this was absolutely monstrous! I was convinced that we had a music that was just as vigorous as anything that America had produced, and we should be pursuing some kind of national identity, not just becoming an arm of American cultural imperialism.

That's the way I saw it, as a political thinker at the time, and it's still the way I see it (1987).'

How this manifested itself in the Singers Clubs in the late 1950s and through to the 1960s was in the issuing of Draconian communiqués setting down in tablets of stone what could and what could not be sung, and by whom, in the Singers Clubs. These were known as 'The Policy Rules' and could not be deviated from on threat of expulsion. MacColl again to Denselow -

'If the singer was English, then the songs had to be from the English tradition. If the singer were American the song had to be American and so on.'

MacColl and Lloyd went even further and a whole string of 'Policy Rules' were issued, this time dealing with the 'style' in which a song could be sung. There were learned debates and communiques about the use of amplification. Even at a Folk festival, it was argued, a 'proper' singer would not use amplification for fear of breaking the 'Policy Rules' on what constituted the correct attitude to performing in a working class setting. This argument would continue until the early 1970s and beyond. In her book *The Imagined Village*, Georgina Boyes points out that as late as 1984 a 'traditional group' encountered problems performing in a Policy Rules club because they used electric instruments. In the 1950s and 60s people arriving with guitars were actually hissed and encouraged to sing unaccompanied. The irony behind all this was that if someone arrived with, or played a concertina they were welcomed, as this was supposedly a 'traditional' instrument!

Evenings in the clubs were fairly rigidly formatted. There would be guest singers, an MC, and an 'open floor' policy. This was a space during the evening for anybody in the audience to get up and sing. New talent was encouraged, but strictly along Policy Rules lines.

To an awful lot of people who simply wanted to listen to music the whole thing had gone beyond a joke. How on earth can a musicologist, or anybody else for that matter, take it upon themselves to prescribe what is a true 'English', or any other style? This inflexible Stalinist approach to a particular genre of music very nearly strangled the Folk Revival just before it reached puberty. The constant Maoist group- and self-criticism, and in-fighting exacted its toll on the nascent Folk scene and discouraged many newcomers, but by the end of the 1950s MacColl and Lloyd had clawed back many members who basically had nowhere else to go. The legacy of Policy Rules continued to play havoc with the English Folk scene for a long time; people having to contend with accusations of 'selling out', and 'going commercial', etc, when all they really wanted to do was broaden their musical horizons. Meanwhile, outside the Singers Clubs, events both social and musical, began to overtake the Folk Revival.

The Post-War Blues Revisited

Post-War England was a dour place. A burst of revolutionary fervor had assaulted the ballot boxes in 1945 and seen the election of a Labour government with a landslide majority. They brought in radical reforms of the social services and the introduction of free health care and pensions and all the other benefits of a welfare state. The economic chaos brought about by the expenditure on World War Two meant that the instant utopia that voters had perceived as coming immediately was not to happen and the next election saw the return of the Tories who were to remain in power for the next thirteen years. Whilst Prime Minister Harold MacMillan may have declared that 'You've never had it so good', the economic stringencies imposed by England's role as defender of freedom during the war still continued to bite. Even those born five years after the war ended can still remember sweet and clothes rationing. Whilst America went through an unprecedented economic boom in terms of consumer goods such as TV's, fridges and cars, in England, hundreds of thousands still had to use outside lavatories. Change was due and change was coming, but it was a slow process.

By the mid 1950s many ordinary young people were able to take advantage of the recent educational reforms and attend university. This figure was to swell during the 1960s. The reason for this was that, prior to the second World War, England boasted only a handful of universities. In the 1950s so-called 'Red Brick', that is newly-built universities, were granted charters, trebling the numbers. Another provision of Higher and Further Education was the founding of Polytechnics and Technical Colleges. By the early 1960s every major town in England had a Polytechnic. Consequently, student numbers mushroomed. There were full-time, part-time and day-release students, some following academic courses and many others vocational. A growing proportion of them were amongst those interested in the Folk Revival, where the bland inanities of Pop music could be counteracted by immersion in the 'true' music of the people. This was particularly strongly felt because pop in England was such a pale imitation of the American Pop scene. Blue jeans, proper denim ones, were almost impossible to get hold of until later on in the 60s. People made do with what passed as the coveted article. Woolworth's sold replica denims. Some people, like Pop artist Peter Blake, bought bibbed blue overalls and cut off the bib and sewed belt loops onto the waist. Others were lucky enough to live in seaports where they could buy them from sailors. Records too. Up until skiffle, guitars were virtually unknown in this country. Even when they became more available, for a long time they were unaffordable; plectrums and strings as rare as gold dust. Harmonica holders were made out of wire coat hangers.

Times were hard, narrow and dull. And a highly educated, increasingly self-aware youth were looking for a way out.

Enter The Young Artist - Stage Right

For many fans and musicians alike, Folk clubs and Folk music offered avenues of exploration outside and beyond the remit of Pop and Beat clubs. For those souls dissatisfied with contemporary Pop, or those becoming more interested in where the music took its spirit from, the world of Folk, rigid as it was in those changing times, was the place to look for knowledge and encouragement. For folk wasn't just the realm of ardent crusading communists, it was a world in which radical ideas were freely exchanged. A sympathy for the goals of nuclear disarmament, a desire to question accepted values, a thirst for information - anything, literature, music, concepts - everything was part and parcel of the explosion in consciousness that was taking place as the shackles of conformity were studied, shaken, then broken. This is where Bob Dylan became supremely important to the lives of a whole generation, because he offered a cornucopia of influences that went way beyond anything experienced before. He became a guide, guru, and mentor for a whole generation of people who hungered for change. When Dylan sang about the Civil Rights struggle in Alabama, as he did in 'Only A Pawn in the Game,' he introduced us to another world, and he enabled us to become part of this world without the need of a visa or a passport. We journeyed to Oxford Town and Selma, Alabama through Dylan's songs.

In addition to the songs themselves, there were the artefacts. It's impossible to explain now to anyone who wasn't around at the time, the importance that would be attached to a Dylan album sleeve, publicity photo, or press article. Here was something that was just as crucial as the Rossetta Stone. An artifact that could be pored over for clues and meanings. A text to be deconstructed in order to find the way. Many of the people I interviewed for this book have stated that the bits of information that they gathered together from Dylan's oeuvre, lyrics, covers, interviews, etc helped bring about fundamental changes in their lives. Ezra Pound and TS Eliot? Dave Van Ronk? Murph the surf? Gertrude Stein? Aztec anthropology? Woody Guthrie? Triumph motorbikes? Einstein and Robin Hood? The motorcycle, black Madonna two-wheeled gypsy queen? Who the hell were Allen Ginsberg, Mike MacClure, Sleepy John Estes? Ma Rainey, Beethoven and a thousand others? Wow man, strictly for the birds! But this was the fountainhead for the grail quest. Who knew where it would lead? And the interesting thing is that it wasn't just the college academics and high school students who found their imaginations fired by this strange, small, mystical rebbe from the mid-west. It was all sorts of people from shop assistants to waiters and maybe even lawyers and crooks who were inspired by his creations to go out and look for more than was being offered them by society.

Enter The Beat - Bed Rolls & Poetry

Beats are an oft-neglected aspect of British youth culture. Mostly what gets fondly remembered these days, or written about in academic texts, is the inevitable Mods and Rockers trip. The Beats were a whole different ballgame.

They began to emerge in the early 1960s and the name 'Beats' originally came from a shortened version of 'Beatnik', the original Bohemians of the 1950s. There is a slight link to the Beat movement, the literary-fuelled American soul searchers like Kerouac and Ginsberg, who professed it to mean 'beat' as in 'beatific', but Beat in Britain developed like the marsupials of Australia. Alone, in isolation, in their own merry way. Pam Lee has suggested that in England the term was derived from the put-down term 'Dead Beats', meaning layabouts, and used almost proudly - like the 70s term Punk.

At a time of more or less full employment, Beats deliberately chose not to work. When necessity forced them into it, they'd take manual jobs on a kind of seasonal basis: fruitpicking; transient farm work; that sort of thing. Jobs that fitted in with their nomadic lifestyle. Work for a few months, then take nine months off and, if they were resident in the UK, supplement what income they had by claiming dole.

What they owned they carried round with them, bedrolls and a pack. Their hair was long - very long by the standards of the time. Sandals and jeans, army surplus jackets, or the long leather jacket as worn by Dylan in *Don't Look Back*. Shades and an attitude were de rigeur. They were proto-type hippies.

Culturally they occupied a kind of mental no man's land in the middle of the growing tribalisation of Mods and Rockers. The Beats didn't care for labelling and embraced anything that turned them on. They could be found at Beat clubs, Folk clubs, or wherever. The ridiculous 'Policy Rules' being pumped out by the Singers Clubs meant nothing to them. Because they travelled so widely the Beats were able to spread knowledge around. Knowledge of what was going down in other cities and knowledge of the kind of music that other people were playing. In their small way they acted as seed carriers for change.

Wherever they went they would talk of Renbourn and Jansch, Ginsberg and Ferlinghetti. They would talk of Dylan too. In December 1962 Dylan had spent a couple of weeks in London and made friends with guitarist Martin Carthy. He'd played at several Folk clubs, including a Peggy Seeger, Ewan MacColl-run Singers Club at the Pindar of Wakefield pub. MacColl and Seeger were distinctly unimpressed, not to say down right hostile, to the young American performer. However, younger members of the audiences at those first British gigs were less stuck-up about tradition-alism and enjoyed their first exposure to Dylan. Word began to spread, and even as far back as then the battle lines were being drawn as regards where you stood in terms of liking or disliking Bob Dylan.

The Beats and other fellow travellers did their bit in turning people on to the phenomenon. Coupled with the chart success of 'Blowing In The Wind,' this ensured that Dylan's name began to spread, not just in Folk clubs but in other cultural arenas too.

The gig at London's Festival Hall which Dylan did a few days after his trip to Didsbury, confirmed him in his status as a rising cult icon. He was being listened to and appreciated by the hiperatti. The Beatles and Stones name checked Dylan in interviews. He was interviewed on BBC radio and appeared on a prime time TV show called 'Tonight'. By the end of 1964 he was rapidly establishing himself with a much wider audience than the incestuous world of Folk would, or could accommodate.

J'Accuse Bob Dylan!

Herein lay a portion of Dylan's 'crime'. He was becoming more and more popular, and to cap it all, he was becoming more and more popular with a non-Folk audience - ergo he had 'sold out'. 'Gone commercial'. In other words, he was rapidly losing his left wing credentials, seeming to have 'sold out' to the capitalist monster. Within British Folk circles there was ardent talk of a 'betrayal', whatever that meant. He no longer belonged to the small clique that inhabited Folk and to many of the Folk world's denizens, that was unforgivable. And when the new recordings emerging from America were excitedly listened to in this country, all the deeply held suspicions were confirmed. Add to this the chart success of Dylan's post-protest period songs such as 'Subterranean Homesick Blues' and you have all the evidence that you need. Dylan was guilty.

Combine all these elements of the constituent parts of a Bob Dylan audience - Folk Traditionalists, teenyboppers, Beats, music fans, and the simply curious - and you get the volatile crowd that waited to greet Dylan in 1966. Trouble was a brewing and trouble would surely come.

The Fatal Flower Garden - The Folk Music Scene In America

The British and American Folk Revivals share many of the same characteristics. Both were rooted in an already existing tradition, both emerged as a conscious or not reaction against the banality of Pop music after the first glow of authentic Rock 'n' Roll had peaked. A final characteristic that they both shared, though this was more deeply felt in America, was a link to political and social change.

Whilst the majority of Americans were basking in the warmth of postwar prosperity a small minority of mainly white, middle class young people were becoming dissatisfied with the conspicuous materialism of what Lyndon Johnson would go on to call 'The Great Society'. There was a deepening awareness in these young people of the problems that simmered below the surface of American life: racial segregation; injustice and inequality.

If everything was supposed to be so great, how come so much was so wrong? The easy answers provided by America's politicians and television pundits no longer carried the same weight as they had done during the golden years of Roosevelt's fireside chats and 'The New Deal'. Towards the end of the 1950s the unique trust that had once existed between the people and the government was slowly and gradually being brought into question.

The incredibly rapid rise of the new phenomenon, 'Youth Culture', must also be taken into account. Within music, at the cinema and in literature, all the old regular answers were being found wanting. There was a restlessness in the air. A growing dissatisfaction. At this point in time there was no counter culture mass movement, just small groups of people dotted here and there, mainly on university campuses and in the big towns, but groups, never the less, who gathered together for their own satisfaction, collecting and making their own music that would come to fruition in the early 1960s.

The revival was a hybrid creature composed of disparate elements of the Old Left, union members, former Lincoln Brigade survivors, and so forth. Plus there was an input from the Jazz avant-garde, and the beatnik, proto-hippies. People were beginning to experiment with marijuana and hallucinogenics, which were at that time still legal. This opening of the 'Doors of Perception' was leading to a dramatic realignment of visionary forces, heralding the dawning of a new era.

From the vast archives of the past there was so much to be drawn on. Harry Smith's *Anthology Of American Folk Music* had come out in 1952, and had introduced a whole new generation of eager listeners to a world that must have seemed a thousand years ago even though, in reality, the material was only around thirty years old. When musicologists like Mike Seeger began looking around they were amazed that many of the performers on Smith's seminal collection were still alive. In England Bill Leader imported each album from the anthology as separate entities on the Topic label. Even in the early 1960s it was common to still find them in the Folk sections of record stores.

When the artists that Dave Laing has called, 'the new interpreters' began emerging in the late 1950s, there was a growing and eager audience awaiting them. The Kingston Trio were the first to pass over into mainstream success, scoring an unlikely Top Ten Hit in 1958 with a 100 year old ballad about a judicial murder entitled 'Hang Down Your Head Tom Dooley,' which had also provided an English hit for Lonnie Donegan. Odetta, and Peter, Paul And Mary, both acts also managed by Albert Grossman, Judy Collins and Joan Baez, The Limelighters and the Chad Mitchell Trio, arose alongside the new-found interest in such rediscovered artists as Sonny Terry and Brownie McGhee, Big Bill Broonzy and Doc Boggs. But even with such a wealth of talent the American Folk Revival was found by some of its stalwarts to be lacking.

Entrenched in their coffeehouses and campuses the American aficionados of the new music were surprised to be told by Folk stalwart Pete Seeger that England was the place to be. He'd toured there in 1961 and came back invigorated and excited by the burgeoning (and presumably highly disciplined) Folk Revival. In 1961, while American singing was still dominated by the American equivalent of the 'Policy Rules', in England, new song-writing was being actively encouraged by Lloyd and others. Modern ballads for modern times was the maxim. Seeger was amazed at how much Folk seemed to have passed over into the English mainstream. In America he was more or less 'blacklisted' because of his political affiliations, whereas in England he was asked to appear on television and radio. Malvina Reynolds, doyen of the American Folk Movement and writer of 'Little Boxes' and The Searchers' hit 'What Have They Done To

The Rain?', even appeared on British TV's top variety show 'Sunday Night At The London Palladium'. Here's Bob Dylan's view of life in the coffee houses circa 1961, taken from Cameron Crowe's liner notes to *Biograph*:

'There was just a clique, you know. Folk Music was a strict and rigid establishment. If you sang Southern Mountain Blues, you didn't sing Southern Mountain Ballads and you didn't sing City Blues. If you sang Texas Cowboy songs, you didn't play English ballads. It was really pathetic.'

It was into this growing milieu that Dylan placed himself, attracted by the disenfranchised, the philosophy and the style of the new, the different. Dylan was among the first to begin blending genres, mixing styles and - Seeger be praised! - writing his own songs, haltingly at first, and then in an astonishingly short period of time, in his own way.

And, in exactly the same way that his new vision would enrage the British, the post-*Times They Are A Changing*-Dylan would infuriate the American upholders of the Traditionalist banner.

CHAPTER THREE
Mixed Up Confusion

From Newport to Dallas, from Newark to Detroit, from Cleveland to San Diego, from Canada to Hawaii, from Australia to Europe, all in nine months (see Appendix 3). Add up all the dates and then take into consideration the time needed to complete *Highway 61 Revisited*, write and record a double album, *Blonde On Blonde*, and, oh yes, get married, and still find the time to hang out with The Beatles, The Stones and go to parties. By any Rock 'n' Roll standards it's a gruelling schedule. This was the maelstrom that Dylan existed in for nearly twelve whole months in the mid 1960s. And throughout this whole period everything just got hotter and hotter - the pressures more and more intense.

On The Road Again

'i accept chaos. i'm not sure whether it accepts me,' Dylan wrote in the liner notes of *Bringing It All Back Home*, throwing a gauntlet in the face of chance, tempting the fates to do with him as they would.

Have you ever been on the road? Have you ever covered the crazy miles of endless highways gazing through a bus window at nothing? You become psychically dislocated, your spirit can't settle. You're stuck in the loop with the Beast and the Beast is always hungry. It demands things, things you wouldn't dream of back in the safety of your home, but you don't have a home anymore. Just an endless chain of hotel rooms, all blurring into one another. Rooms that the Beast claims as his own territory, stalking through your chamber with his two of his Daemons, Sleep, and Nosleep.

Daemon Sleep is a trickster who fools you into thinking you're safe, but when you wake up, still without enough sleep, well, you just don't know where you are. Then, through the fog of threshold awakening you realise that even though you're not sure where you are, you know for certain that wherever it is, ain't where it's at.

Nosleep is the Beast's darkest childe and squats by the side of your head as you lie tossing and turning, whispering, pleading, imploring, sabotaging and despoiling the rest your body screams for. Nosleep's big trick is to let you drift off just as it's time to get up. Nosleep has a confederate and ally in a human agency known as 'speed', and the seeds that they sow together lead to unreason.

Imagine spending most of your time being moved from place to place. Time zones shift. One day it's spring, the next it's winter and back again, in as long as it takes you to climb aboard a Lodestar 13 seater aircraft, or a coach built for thirty. There are no Walkmans, no inflight (or coach) videos, no chemical toilets. Hell, when NASA got the first men on the moon four years later there weren't even digital clocks! All you can do is do what you can. You can read if the ride ain't too bumpy. You can talk if there's anything new to be said. You can't even rap about the towns you've been in because you didn't spend long enough in any of them to form a coherent opinion. Hell, one hour extra in a town finding the time to eat a hamburger is a novelty! Superficiality and necessity breed a form of closeness, but even the bonds of friendship can't beat the Boredom and its overwhelming angst. Boredom is a mother of a weight to carry and the temptation put in your way by the Beast is to fight the Boredom with an ever-increasing envelope of insularity.

Just look at Dylan's press conferences during that year.

Sydney Airport, April 12th, 66:

Q - How would you describe yourself?

Dylan - I don't describe myself. How do you describe yourself?

Q - I have no idea.

And so it went. From London -May 23rd, 66:

Q - Who do you think is the best folksinger in the world?

Dylan - Oh, Peter Lorre.

To Paris,

May 23rd, 66:

Q - Are you happy?

Dylan - Yes, as an ashtray perhaps....

Bob and his entourage knew what he was talking about even if half the population of the Lower East Side and the rest of the world didn't. Within the bounds of our language lies our ability to practice defence against a foe that we cannot even measure.... And maybe even a foe that isn't really there.

This Motel Ain't Big Enough For The Twenty Of Us

Stick twenty or so souls within a specific environment, a hot house say, or a culture jar, and watch the fun. Allegiances form, alliances are forged and eventually enemies are made. That physical closeness, the being penned up with one another day in and day out helps familiarity breed contempt. You can't make friends with strangers, not for more than a couple of hours anyway, and though they're staying where they are, you in your orbital ellipse have to move on and out. Outlaw blues.

Throughout Dylan and The Hawks' American leg of the tour the entourage encompassed the souls of up to twenty hapless persons, all of them signed on in blood. Having taken, what we in England would call 'the King's shilling', those blessed with Bob's benediction engaged upon an enterprise that haplessly mirrors Melville's titanic American novel *Moby Dick*. The analogy here relates to the tale of a crew of various persons caught up in the mighty quest of one man in pursuit of the impossible.

Dig the film script -

'Call Me... Robbie Robertson.'

Dylan, as Ahab, single minded in his frantic chase of that thin, wild, mercury music.

The camera pans over Greenwich Village, for it is from these mythologised surroundings that the guys get the beat (even if we know they're from Canada!). The Great White Whale is the 'Mathematical Music' that

Dylan speaks so fondly of in 65/66. The Pequod is the Tour itself. A relentless juggernaut that propels its crew with fatalistic abandon around the world. On the way sailors jump ship, Helm and Kooper being amongst the first to leave. Terrified of the quest? Enraptured of the trail? We'll never know. Kooper had 'differences', Helm just grew tired of the booing and couldn't take it anymore. Bobby Gregg came next, then Sandy Konikoff. His replacement, Micky Jones, came from a fine tradition of American Popular Music. He'd played with Trini Lopez, then went to Dylan and ended up with Kenny Rogers. It's a good job that he didn't stay with the mad 'If I Had A Hammer', Loony Toons precursor of the folk boom, Lopez, because he's the best damn drummer that Dylan ever had playing live for him. Micky Jones is at the prow of the whaleboat, harpoon in hand, beating out the tattoo of the fin and the tail, punctuating the rhythm of the waves with the heartbeat of his hands: forever Queequeg in John Huston's movie. Rick Danko is Starbuck and an unlikely Albert Grossman takes over the part of the preacher, Mapple, played by Orson Welles in Huston's film. 1956 has caught up with the reality of 1965 when these impressionable young men were pressed on board. It was 'All aboard!' and 'What a long, strange trip it's been!'. Stand by for the Mighty Quinn.

Some Practicalities & Inconsequentialities

For short hauls on the American leg of the tour, a pilot and co-pilot to fly the Lodestar ('Jet Pilot'/'Pilot Eyes'?), for long hauls they flew commercial. Dylan, Victor, Albert, Bobby. Two roadies to truck the gear, Henri to take care of the guitars, Tom to drive the limos. Robbie, Rick, Richard, Garth, Levon, Bobby, Sandy or Mickey. Robert Van Dyke, Bob Alderman, Bill Avis, Phil Ramone, and then, when they hit Europe, add DA Pennebaker, Howard and Jones Alk and UK/Columbia Gofer, Fred Perry. Plus guests.

The logistics are frightening. Food, accommodation, travel, drugs, all worked out in minute detail, no room for error. Timetables, schedules, soundchecks, all this was more or less uncharted territory in the mid 60s. Many of the venues, certainly in England, had never hosted large scale rock concerts before. After Dylan and The Hawks, many wished they'd never have to again. The Free Trade Hall had played host to a whole variety of concerts and events. The world famous Halle Orchestra was based there. Jazz concerts featuring performers such as Count Basie and Duke Ellington were regular fixtures. School choirs and classical quartets, but never, never before had they had an evening like Dylan and his travelling circus of freaks and electricity.

The gear that Dylan's roadies were hauling around the world was state of the art American technology costing over $30,000 [a veritable King's ransom at today's prices]. It was huge. There were big black bin speakers piled on top of one another at each side of the band. There were box shaped foldback monitors positioned all over the stage, some angled directly at Dylan. On the sides were arrows pointing up and the words, 'handle with care' stencilled on them. Microphones, cables, guitar amps, organ amp, all being pumped out through the PA at 1000 watts. The rest of the rock world didn't start using rigs this big for another two or three years.

Running Through The Jungle

There's another bizarre comparison to be drawn here. An unlikely parallel with the activities of another group of young Americans in another place that's far away from home - and that place was Vietnam. They carted off their technology there too, all shiny and new. Bigger than everyone else's. Several witnesses to the 66 tour have remarked on the sound of Dylan and The Hawks blasting the second set open with 'Tell Me Momma' being like that of a B52 taking off, the sheer weight of the sound pushing you back in your seat like as if it was an actual physical force. Nine years later we get an indirect 'Nam reference with the Rolling Thunder Tour. Rolling Thunder, an expression originally taken from a hymn, was the name given to saturation carpet bombing of Vietnam by B52s. Dylan told Robert Shelton that he had looked up in the sky and heard a booming sound and decided to call the 1975 tour Rolling Thunder. Whatever. Back in 1966 American technology was busy on two continents and, if some critics are to be taken seriously, both actions were acts of cultural imperialism. Too many young men, high on their mission. Too many young men high on the reds, the whites and the blues.

The tour becomes Dylan's equivalent of a Search and Destroy operation, deep into the heart of darkness. Each tune a Zippo raid on the sensibilities of perceived taste. Each concert hall a landing zone. You almost expect the purple smoke as they hit the stage running. Robertson's staccato guitar bursts, rapid fire. Jones' drums, the throbbing beat of air support. Danko and Manuel, helpless grunts, following their LT anywhere into the impenetrable jungle.

Whatever the analogies, the PA remains a problem throughout the tour.

'I Think It Was A Little Loud In The Second Half.'

In Vermont, a reporter wrote -

'A muddy amplification system with too much volume prevented many of the audience from hearing the words to some of the songs...'

In Toronto -

'The Big Sound (capitals in original) drowns out all his message...'

And back to Vietnam again from *Macleans Magazine* -

'At Dylan's signal, Levon and the Hawks exploded into sound like a squadron of jet planes, a leaping, rising, crushing wave of sound that pulsed the air and rocked the floor...'

Jules Siegel in *Saturday Evening Post* reported that Dylan too was aware of problems with the PA. He wrote about an incident he witnessed in a hotel after a gig on the West Coast when Dylan confronted a dozing Albert Grossman -

'"Al-bert," Dylan cried, "Albert, did you hear that? They couldn't hear me Al-bert, I mean they couldn't hear me. What good is it if they can't hear me? We've got to get that sound man out here to fix it. What do you think Albert?"

'Grossman stirred on the bed and answered soothingly, "I told you in the car that the volume was too high. Just cut the volume by about a third and it'll be all right." Grossman went back to sleep, very much like an occidental Buddha, snoring lightly. Dylan was satisfied.'

Siegel also reports that Grossman had to run on stage on more than one occasion to tell Dylan to stop 'eating the mike', which was adding to the problems of reverberation.

'Man, that was just terrible,' Dylan is reported as saying at one point on the American leg. There then followed a serious debate with Grossman on the expediency of playing arenas instead of theatres on the next jaunt,

Australia. Grossman persuaded Dylan that Australia being 'underdeveloped' didn't have enough concert halls, so arenas it had to be.

By the time Dylan and his legion of the damned arrived in Manchester the stage was already set for something climactic. Reports had been filtering back to England since Newport in July 1965, though the debate had raged since long before then.

More Folk Music Shit

Had Dylan 'sold out?' Had he 'gone commercial?'

These were arguments furiously debated in the cellar that was the Ladybarn Folk Club in late 1964. Ted Pugh, intense Celtic traditionalist had nearly come to blows with Paul Watson, proud owner of a restored Steel National. This was before anything electric had even been released, but they could tell. The purists scented blood in the wind when they first heard *Another Side Of Bob Dylan*, with its rambling incoherencies and 'pop' oriented slants weakly varnishing over romanticised imagery (their views!).

How could the man who wrote 'With God On Our Side' come up with 'All I Really Wanna Do?' Why didn't he just get back to doing what he did properly, and save the world by writing protest songs? Of course, Irwin Silber in his open letter to Dylan in November's *Sing Out* had voiced many of the same concerns, accusing Dylan of having become, 'inner-directed', 'inner probing', 'a little maudlin', and that all he seemed to be doing was, 'relating to a handful of cronies behind the scenes'. Adding as a coda, 'The paraphernalia of fame is getting in your way'.

By the spring of 1965 all Hell broke loose when Dylan released *Bringing It All Back Home*. To the purists, and there were many though they would hold their fire and keep their powder dry until the 66 tour, the gauntlet had been well and truly flung down.

'Maggie's Farm,' 'Outlaw Blues,' and, worst of all, a chart hit with 'Subterranean Homesick Blues,' were cultural dynamite with the kind of audience Dylan had at that time. What those songs did was extend his wider fanbase, but that process was still in the early stages. When Dylan arrived in England for his concert tour in May 1965 most of the interest was still from his older fans and there was an air of expectation as regards what he'd be performing and whom he'd be performing it with. As it worked out, the war hadn't yet started, but it wasn't far off. Dylan busked his way through England avoiding controversy by playing a kind of greatest hits package, solo. By all accounts, when he returned to America he was disgusted at the ease of it all, the fact that the concerts no longer presented a challenge to him, and that audiences were too accepting. He told Robert Shelton that he was sick of playing at being 'Bob Dylan,' and added to Nat Hentoff:

'I knew what was going to happen all the time, y'know? I knew how many encores there was, which kind of songs they were going to clap loudest at and all this kind of thing'.

If those stories are true then it leads to the creation of one of the greatest songs of all time, 'Like A Rolling Stone.' There are reports that Dylan flirted with the idea of retiring from performing and even writing music, to concentrate exclusively on poetry and literature. Whatever, on his return from England, after a bout of sickness and a stay in a London hospital, he began to write the lyrics for this historic masterpiece, describing it as page after page of a 'long piece of vomit', that all had to come out of his mixed-up confusion. If the impetus for it was derived from his English tour, it was certainly to England that he brought it all home a year later. By the bucketful.

By that time, of course, the anger and cynicism of 'Like A Rolling Stone' had been fed and fuelled by the reaction that the tour was getting around the globe. It had all started at Newport, Mecca of the American Folk Revival.

Ladies And Gentlemen - Mr Bob Dylan

The festival was held in Newport's Freebody Park on Rhode Island, and attracted at the time of Dylan's first appearance, 46,000 people, mainly young, white college kids, roughly the same age as Dylan. They were there, as they had been in increasing numbers for the last couple of years, to celebrate the emergent folk tradition and the rising tide of young and not so young performers who appeared there in workshops and concert sessions. Newport went hand in hand with the newly emerging Civil Rights movement. It was, in essence, a reflection of the idealism of Kennedy's new era: the troubadours and minstrels of Camelot gathered together in one place, at one time. A coming together of the 'second New Dealers', or, more accurately, the liberal baby boomers. A fusion of the concerned, the disillusioned and the curious. Newport had long hosted a jazz and blues festival that acted as a kind of catalyst, or crucible, for alternatives to the mainstay showbiz and pop world of American mass culture. Now the folk movement of the early 60s was itself acting as a catalyst for the nurturing of new forms of music and the new talent that played it.

When Dylan first hit there in 1963 his star was on the ascendant. Dylan's was the name on everybody's lips at Newport - audience and performers. Even before he came on stage it was uttered or announced countless times by singers and players as they began versions of his songs. When he finally appeared for his own solo set on Friday evening it was to a standing ovation. He was brought back at the end of the night's concert and joined such luminaries of the folk movement as Pete Seeger, Theodore Bikel, Peter, Paul and Mary, Joan Baez and The Freedom Singers, in linking arms and singing 'We Shall Overcome'. The crowd near enough tore the place to pieces (in a non-violent sort of way).

When Dylan returned in 1964 he had almost assumed godhead. To many in the Newport crowd he was a deity, sanctified and beatified by the adulation heaped upon him by the adoring audience, not just at Newport, but all over the world. But even in 1964 there were mutterings about his approach and new found style. What we have here is a singer who has gone outside and beyond the folk schemata of the American revival and is flying into a whole new realm beyond.

Perhaps A Little Too Much Mercury?

Listening to Dylan's performance at Newport in 1964, you get a sense of a man who is certainly stoned. The phrasing is a shade too relaxed. The harmonica playing on 'Mr Tambourine Man' in particular, hesitant and dare one say it - lazy? If you compare it to other performances of this anthem that he gave that year or even a year later, Newport does seem to be coming from somewhere else. A couple of unconcerned fluffs with the words betray Dylan's state of mind. This is not an amphetamined gig. Rather, it suggests marijuana and Wild Turkey. The ennui and boredom that would sit on Dylan's shoulders in the year to come is here, crawling slowly up the length of his spine. Unobtrusively making its way upwards, the better to whisper in his ear.

Dave Van Ronk and others claim that Dylan's problems may even have been in evidence the year before. Dylan was building walls around himself even then, walking around the grounds of the festival motel flicking a twenty-foot long bullwhip. According to Anthony Scaduto in his book *Bob Dylan* (the first serious Dylan biography), a young contemporary of Dylan's had already noticed something else about him:

'You could begin to sense the fear. Bobby was touched by a fear of it all, starting back there at Newport when it all began to get together for him'.

All of which brings us to whatever fear Dylan must have been feeling in 1965 at Newport, when he was about to unleash on the festival a new, re-invented Dylan. A Dylan that was undertaking another journey into the unknown - Electricity.

The essential sound had been formatted in two studios, the 30th Street and Columbia's Studio A, starting in December 1964. Alongside producer Tom Wilson, Dylan had begun the search for a sound that would be uniquely his. *Bringing It All Back Home* would be the result of this first experiment. The journey into 'mathematical music' would continue in Studio A on June 15 and 16. After hauling his new found 'style' onto the Newport stage, Dylan returned to the studio for four more sessions which would culminate in the release of *Highway 61 Revisited* at the end of August 1965.

'Like A Rolling Stone' was cut on June 16 and released four weeks later. By August it had reached number 2 in the Billboard chart, the highest position Dylan was to ever attain. The song's character and texture in both its style and content appear to have been exactly what Dylan was looking for, and the motley crew of musicians Dylan and his new producer, Bob Johnston, had gathered together for the sessions were becoming singularly adept at creating the right alchemical fusion. The time was now right for Dylan to unveil his 'new sound'.

Fate, synchronicity, or whatever, placed the Newport Festival slap bang in the middle of the sessions, and one of the musicians, guitarist Mike

Bloomfield, was to be there performing with his regular outfit, The Paul Butterfield Blues Band. Taking former Royal Teens guitarist and songwriter (who can ever forget 'Short Shorts'?), Al Kooper, who had accidently provided the organ work on 'Like A Rolling Stone,' and pianist Barry Goldberg along for the ride, the Pope of Folk headed towards Newport with mischief in mind.

A Man With A Mission

It's worth trying to put ourselves inside Dylan's shoes (for just one moment!). Here was a young man who, just several months before, had felt terminally bored with what he had become. It was all too easy doing what he had been doing, his creativity had been questioned by his own worst critic, himself. On his return from England he had felt like retiring from music altogether, but then something had exploded inside his head and given him a completely new direction. He was now fuelled by the new music he could hear inside his head - music which was already beginning to take shape in the studio.

' "Rolling Stone" is the best song I wrote,' Dylan told Ralph J Gleason in an interview for *Ramparts* Magazine ... 'I wrote "Rolling Stone" after England. I boiled it all down, but it's all there. I had to quit after England. I had to stop and I knew I had to sing it with a band ...'

'No man,' Dylan is reported as saying to a friend at the time. 'Amphetamine doesn't help me write songs, it just helps me stay up longer to write more of them.'

... Dylan was on a high. The power of the songs emerging from Studio A screams this out. There is a famous photograph taken around this time by Daniel Kramer: Dylan is at a piano in the studio, punching both arms into the air at the end of a take. The grin on his face is somehow uncharacteristic of the songwriter. We've never seen him this happy before. It's strange and almost out of place, but the expression on his face cannot be denied. Dylan is ecstatic, and the vibrancy and energy of the songs on *Bringing It All Back Home* and *Highway 61 Revisited* is testimony to the excitement we are witness to, even thirty-odd years later. This music shines and rings clear like a bell. It is a clarion call to the new age. No wonder Dylan wanted to take his new noble anthems and perform them for his people, the ones who had blessed him with their benediction three years before: to return to Newport and give of himself his visions and dreams unto the crowd that had greeted him so warmly before. So, he did, and the crowd was hardly grateful.

Drawing Down The Moon

Or were they? So far after the event people are beginning to call into question the testimony surrounding Newport. On the evidence of surviving audio tapes the crowd seem to be politely, if a tad reservedly applauding Dylan. Certainly their appreciation is more marked after the electric set, but what we have to bear in mind is that this is a soundboard recording and the audience was, if at all, only miked up minimally. Whatever the veracity of contemporary historians and re-evaluations of existing evidence, the reports that emanated from Newport, and certainly the reports that we received over here in England, were that Dylan had got a rough ride and a rocky reception for his electric set from the American crowd.

Newport 1965 represented the contemporary American Folk scene in microcosm. The old guard of the Revival were there in force: Jean Ritchie, Pete Seeger, Alan Lomax. For them the festival was the summation of all they'd worked towards. Newport was not just an open air concert, but a celebration of the world of folk music: in addition to the main musical attractions, workshop stages were dotted around the site. Throughout the weekend you could watch the acts on the main stage or take part in sessions about worksongs, spirituals or banjo picking. You could even watch Pete Seeger and a group of ex-convicts chopping wood while singing genuine chain gang songs in time with their axe strokes.

But another force was also there for the weekend, younger, hungrier, hipper, upstart kids who had taken and learnt from the old guard but who were now looking for other ways of musically expressing themselves: people like Dylan's old friends Ric Von Schmidt, Mimi and Dick Farina, Maria Muldaur and the Jim Kweskin Jug Band.

Looking at photographs taken that year at Newport, the divisions of age and political versus personal freedom become more apparent. Pete Seeger has on a denim workshirt and stout boots. Country artists like Byron Berline and the Charles River Boys wear the required white shirts, bootlace ties and matching waistcoats. The embryonic freaks, like Muldaur and Farina, are dressed in looser, more unconventional outfits. Men and women wear their hair longer.

This is an important issue, for dress at Newport was a statement of ideology. Folk musicians were expected to wear 'work clothes'. Indeed Lightning Hopkins was said to have arrived at the festival one year in a brand new Cadillac wearing a bright Mohair suit, before changing into overalls and barefeet to take to the stage. This was clearly a game that Dylan would not play.

Joe Boyd was stage manager and remembers his arrival:

'There was a tremendous anticipation at Newport about Dylan - "Is he here yet?" "Has he arrived?" - and instead of this blue-jeaned, work-shirted guy who'd arrived in 1964 to be the pied piper, he arrived rather secretively ... And they (Dylan's entourage) were all wearing puff-sleeved duelling shirts - one of them was polka dot - and they were not wearing blue jeans ... They wore sunglasses. The whole image was very, very different ...'

All the clannishness, the secrecy and the radical imagery would be perceived as confrontational by the die-hard Traditionalists who were already suspicious of Dylan.

All was well on the Saturday the 24 July. Dylan appeared at an afternoon workshop and performed 'All I Really Want To Do' and 'Mr Tambourine Man.' The crowd was suitably enthusiastic. There is a film of the gig included in the movie *Festival*, a documentary about Newport from 1963 to 1966. Dylan was doing what the average folk fan would have expected of him, that is to say, performing acoustically. On the Sunday, however, things were to be remarkably different.

Bloomfield, as stated earlier, was there with the Butterfield Blues Band. They were scheduled to play on the Sunday afternoon, with Dylan following in the evening. On the Saturday night, Dylan, accompanied by Goldberg and Kooper, rehearsed with Jerome Arnold on bass, and Sam Lay, drummer, also from the Butterfield Blues Band, and the other three musicians, all through the night. Al Kooper recalls that 'It was tiring, but fun.' By the next evening they were ready to go.

During the Sunday afternoon, Dylan, resplendent in tight tapered black pants, black suede Cuban heeled boots, Ray-Bans and a green polka dot shirt, had prowled the back stage area in Freebody Park. For a while he sat with Albert Grossman nervously chain-smoking while on-stage the Butterfield Blues Band provoked a stir in the audience with their renditions of electric Chicago blues numbers. Such was the sacrosanct atmosphere of Newport that any form of electrified instrumentation was regarded with deep suspicion. The festival board had been highly dubious of the merits of letting Butterfield play, but finally capitulated and decided to demonstrate their liberal tendencies by allowing it this once. Although the condescending way in which Alan Lomax introduced them angered the band.

Butterfield Blues band singer Nick Gravenites remembers:

'It was kind of, well, we've got these white guys from Chicago and they say they play blues. Well, let's call 'em up here and see if they can really do it.'

According to Mike Bloomfield, Grossman was so incensed with Lomax's introduction that in an angry confrontation he called him 'a real prick,' causing the two men to end up in a fistfight, 'rolling in the dirt.'

The Butterfield Blues band got a very mixed reception, and years later Bloomfield was still angry at the band's treatment at Newport. He told Tom Yates:

'What we played was music that was entirely indigenous to the neighbourhood, to the city we grew up in. There was no doubt in my mind that this was folk music; this was what I heard on the streets of my city, out the windows, on radio stations and jukeboxes in Chicago and all throughout the South, and it was what people listened to. And that's what folk art meant to me - what people listened to.'

Neither the audience nor the festival board expected to see the band again: they had no idea that Dylan was to use them as backing musicians for his headlining appearance later that day.

Dylan got changed for the set. Sharp black leather jacket and dress shirt, but what he carried on-stage with him that night was intensely more symbolic than any Carnaby Street/Mod clothing. It was a solid body, electric Fender guitar. Kooper, Bloomfield and the others slouched on-stage after him, a roadie plugged him in and the rough-hewn ensemble blasted off into a searing, twisted version of 'Maggie's Farm,' that owed more to Chicago boogie than it did to Dylan. Bloomfield's lead dominates the proceedings, rendering Goldberg and Kooper almost redundant. People began to boo. There was shouting and heckling.

The orthodox version of events is that the Traditionalists in the crowd were outraged and bewildered by what they saw as Dylan's denial of his heritage - his effrontery in desecrating the sanctified ground of Newport with, of all things, mindless rock 'n' roll. Somebody did shout out, 'Go back to the Sullivan show!' and beyond any doubt, people did boo, but there were factors other than Dylan's alleged 'sell out' at play here.

Firstly, Al Kooper believes the crowd may have booed because, 'the band screwed up "Maggie's Farm". That was embarrassing.' However, the more widely recognised cause of the controversy was again the PA.

Joe Boyd told Jonathan Morley in *The Telegraph* No 37:

'... I mean, by today's standards it wasn't very loud, but by those standards of the day it was the loudest thing anybody had ever heard. ... As soon as I had gotten the stage set, I ran around to the press enclosure which was the front section, press and friends and people, and stood sort of at the door of the gates, and watched at the side of the stage, and I thought, "This is great!" ... Somebody pulled at my elbow and said, "You'd better go backstage, they want to talk to you." So I went backstage and there I was confronted by Seeger and Lomax and, I think, Theodore Bikel or somebody, saying, "It's too loud! You've got to turn it down! It's far too loud! We can't have it like this. It's just unbearably loud!" ... I said, "Well, I don't control the sound ..."'

Joe made his way to the sound box,

'... By this time I think it was the beginning of the second number, and there was Grossman and Neuwirth and Yarrow and Rothschild all sitting at the sound desk, grinning, very very pleased with themselves, and meanwhile the audience was going nuts ... There were arguments between people sitting next to each other! Some people were booing, some people were cheering ...'

Backstage Alan Lomax, Pete Seeger and others allegedly tried to cut the power cable with an axe that Seeger had been using for a demonstration of worksongs. Pete Yarrow and others managed to stop them. But the seeds of confusion had already been sown.

Dylan led the group into an exploration of a very embryonic 'Like A Rolling Stone,' although the definitive Bobby Gregg drum smash intro and Kooper's staccato organ riff were missing from the Newport performance. They'd return later in the year as the sound grew more solidified. Onstage that warm Sunday night in 1965, Dylan was only beginning to feel his way around the sound that he wanted live. Also, with the song only having been out for a few days it's unlikely that many in the crowd would have been familiar with the density of lyrics and intensity of emotion that ran through it. More people began booing.

Ric Von Schmidt gave Anthony Scaduto his version of events:

'What happened was, whoever was controlling the mikes messed it up. You couldn't hear Dylan. It looked like he was singing with the volume off... We were sitting in the press section, maybe thirty yards back, and yelling, "Can't hear ya!" and "Cut the band down!"... Then they went into the next song and no one had changed any dials. It was the same thing, no voice coming through at all ...'

In his own bizarre manner, Dylan supported this view in an interview with Norma Ephron and Susan Edmiston:

'They twisted the sound. They didn't like what I was going to play and they twisted the sound on me before I began.'

Dylan finished his set with 'Phantom Engineer', an early up-tempo version of 'It Takes A Lot To Laugh, It Takes A Train To Cry.' Again Bloomfield dominates the proceedings with his strident Chicago boogie guitar. The song ends. Dylan shouts, 'Let's go man. That's all!' Some who were backstage reported that Dylan came off with tears in his eyes, distraught at the reception he'd been given by the crowd. Dylan himself denied this to Scaduto, claiming that he was just stunned and 'a little bit drunk.' Whatever, Dylan left the Newport audience in uproar.

Again though, Al Kooper has an interesting alternative interpretation of events:

'I don't think they were booing us. I think they were just short changed time-wise, and reacting to that. I would if I were them. They booed at the

end because we only played for 15 minutes and everyone else played for 45... and Dylan was the headliner as well.'

Pete Yarrow tried to salvage something from the fiasco. You can hear him on the audio recording. That there is too much confusion is beyond doubt. He came on stage to try and calm things down, but with little success. The audience hubbub punctuates his attempts.

'Bobby was... Yes, he will do another tune if you call him back.... Would you like Bobby to sing another song?'

The reaction to this rather redundant question resembles that of lions being asked if they'd like another Christian. Flummoxed, Yarrow stumbles on...

'I don't know if... Listen, it's the fault of....'

What was he about to say? Was he going to blame the committee?

'He was told he could only do a certain period of time.... Bobby can you do another song please?'

The audience are now chanting, 'We want Dylan! We want Dylan!'

'He's going to get his axe.... He's coming... He's gone to get an acoustic guitar.... Bobby's coming on now...'

The crowd's chanting grows noisier.

'Yes, I understand... that's the case... We want Bobby and we do.... The time problem has meant that he could do only these two songs...'

What does he mean? Dylan had played three songs. Does he mean that Dylan will perform two more? If so, has all this been pre-arranged?

'He'll be out as soon as he can get his acoustic guitar...'

There is a cheer and Dylan returned to the stage.

Chaos and confusion still reigned however as Dylan asked for another guitar which takes a little while to reach him. When it finally did, and he had finished tuning up, he went straight into 'It's All Over Now, Baby Blue,' a performance that many have interpreted as his farewell to Newport, followed by 'Mr Tambourine Man.' He got a standing ovation.

He left the stage and never returned to Newport. From now on Dylan would play it his way, or not at all.

CHAPTER FOUR
Outlaw Blues

Through August 1965 till May 1966 the ship of fools sailed on, Captain Dylan at the helm. Several years later Robbie Robertson told Al Aronowitz in the *Saturday Evening Post* -

'We played some jobs with Bob where the music was sailing - and he was sailing. It turned out to be not just songs. It turned out to be a whole dynamic experience. We did it until we just couldn't do it anymore. We went all over the place until finally it was about ready to burst.'

It was a unique experience. It's almost impossible to think of any other Popular Music performer who had to educate his audience into a new way of listening to things.

Pop icons shifting from the charts to film, and then onwards to 'all-round entertainer' status, had become the accepted route of teen idols. Elvis Presley laid down the parameters for Rock in the 1950s, but then switched completely from sneering, rebel King of Cool, into wholesome family entertainer. This shift, engineered by Colonel Tom Parker, was very much in keeping with the showbiz mores of the time. Parker knew that Popular singers have a relatively short shelf life and the corridors of Pop are littered with the corpses of 'one-hit wonders'. So we saw the change from the Blue Suede Shoes Elvis to the Blue Hawaii Elvis, and this did not result in crowds of people booing him or walking out. But Elvis' change of direction was a career decision, rather than an artistic one. He certainly wasn't betraying a way of life, or a set of values, be-cause rock 'n' roll simply didn't have such a thing.

What Dylan was doing was dangerous because for many he was re-garded as a guru and not a pop idol. It wasn't just a change of style - it was a complete transformation of intent. A more relevant comparison would be with Miles Davis when he turned from jazz to rock fusion in the late sixties.

In his autobiography Miles had this to say:

'All of a sudden jazz became passé, something dead that you put under a glass in the museum and study... I was already moving towards a guitar sound in my music, because I was beginning to listen to a lot of James Brown, and I liked the way he used the guitar in his music. Now I was starting to think about other ways I could approach music I wanted to play... I could feel myself starting to want to change, but I didn't really know yet what this change was all about. I knew that it had something to do with the guitar voice in my music and I was beginning to get interested in what electrical instrumental voicing could do in my music.'

Replace the word jazz for folk, and James Brown for whoever, and this could be Dylan talking. But while Miles Davis was one of the major jazz musicians of the century and the epitome of jazz cool, by the late sixties jazz was so marginalised that the outrage that Miles' 'betrayal' provoked was heard only from a coterie of elite fans and critics. There would be no riots because his was not a mass art form. Dylan's pursuit of 'electrical in-strumental voicing' would be a much harder path.

Playboy Magazine asked Dylan if he thought he'd made a mistake changing his style.

'A mistake is to commit a misunderstanding. There could be no such thing, anyway, as this action. Either people understand or they pretend to understand - or else they really don't understand ...'

Victory Seemed But A Moment Away

It certainly seemed that way at his first gig after Newport, Forest Hills. It was cold for late August and raining intermittently too. All 15,000 seats were sold and Dylan was determined that everything should go right. The backing band, this time consisting of Harvey Brooks, Al Kooper, Levon

Helm and Robbie Robertson, spent two weeks at Bob Carroll's rehearsal rooms, perfecting an electric set that Dylan hoped would show people the sounds he'd been hearing inside his head for nearly a year. The basic format of the show that Dylan devised, a forty-five minute acoustic opening set followed by an electric set of roughly the same length, became the standard for the next eight months.

Dylan and Grossman arrived at Forest Hills at two in the afternoon. He spent a few minutes talking to fans who'd started gathering there earlier in the day and then went off into huddled consultation with the musicians and sound crew. A light squall drove them into the refectory where, over sandwiches and coffee, he had a conversation with photographer Daniel Kramer. He complained to Kramer about how things were getting out of hand with too many demands being made on his time. There were too many things to do: an album to be recorded; *Tarantula*, his novel for MacMillan's had to be finished; he was making plans for a TV special with ABC; and on top of that he was still committed to doing live gigs. He talked about restrictions on his freedom. According to Kramer, he knew that he'd have to give something up in order to make a compromise with this reality. Then the rain stopped and they all walked out to the stage.

Forest Hills is a huge open-air tennis stadium and a stage had been built at one end of the tennis court facing a gigantic horseshoe of seats. Huge speaker bins had been set up facing the crowd. A mountain of mikes, amps, keyboards and cables had been brought in to ensure that there'd be no repetition of Newport's audio problems. This time the audience would be able to hear every word clearly and distinctly as Dylan presented his case for 'mathematical music'.

Albert Grossman personally supervised every detail of rigging the gig, half a dozen crew running round as he barked instructions into a walkie-talkie. Throughout the afternoon, Dylan and the musicians soundchecked and soundchecked again in order to achieve the right balance. For a while they had trouble with the mikes - wind blowing over them made rushing sounds that impaired the clarity - but eventually Dylan and Grossman were satisfied.

After weeks of preparation they were ready.

Ladies And Gentlemen - Murry The K!

When the concert eventually started it was dark and windy. Spotlights pierced the darkness and illuminated the stage. On tapes of the show the crowd sound friendly but feisty. First on to introduce the man who was going to introduce Bob Dylan, was a local DJ called Gary Stevens. He gets a bit of good natured badinage from the crowd, but when the next MC, Murry The K, takes the stage there is something a bit unsettling about the reception he gets. The crowd starts booing Murry and this is almost a portent of what will come later in the evening. I have to keep reminding myself when I listen to the recording that these people haven't been penned in for hours on end, made to stand and be crushed together. OK, it's not a balmy August evening, but they are sat down in the bleachers, nobody's late on stage, everything is running fine. Sure, there would be an air of anticipation, a desire to see the man they've gathered together for, but the atmosphere is edgy, as if Newport has programmed them for a confrontation and Murry and Gary are the warm-up, the lions' hors-d'oeuvres.

After a rambling monologue spiked with the pseudo hip argot of the time Murry gives way to Stevens again and he finally introduces Dylan who gets a rapturous welcome. Equipped solely with his acoustic guitar and harmonica Dylan launches straight into 'She Belongs To Me.' The playing throughout the first half is exemplary Dylan and the tunes chosen represent a writer at the peak of perfection. Five of the songs are off *Bringing It All Back Home*, one ('To Ramona') off *Another Side*, and he premieres a new number, 'Desolation Row,' that will be released on *Highway 61 Revisited* three days later. The audience is enthusiastic. In a sense, reprising his last act at Newport, Dylan finishes off the acoustic section of the show with 'It's All Over Now Baby Blue' and 'Mr Tambourine Man.' The first half over with, Dylan goes backstage to have a pep talk with the boys in the band.

Dylan warned them to expect anything. He told them that the audience might heckle and boo, but that they weren't to let that bother them, they just had to carry on playing and play as best they could. Al Kooper recalls:

'At Forest Hills the lemmings had read in every paper that they were supposed to boo if Dylan played electric, so they did. Bob admonished us just to keep playing no matter what happened.'

This interval represents an interesting moment and it allows us a brief insight into what must have been going through Dylan's mind at the time. He's already experienced Newport and is aware of the levels of animosity his new strange trip is generating, but he is first and foremost an artist - an artist who refuses to compromise his integrity for one second. So in this recess, Dylan is preparing himself for battle on a psychic plain. Very few performers would have risked so much. In 1965 Dylan was on top of the world with a specific winning formula. All of a sudden he appeared to want to throw it all away.

There is another element here that is worthy of some consideration: Albert Grossman who, so it appears, supported Dylan to the hilt, when any normal 'showbiz' manager would have tried every possible way of making the artist keep within their genre. Not Grossman. Here was a man who for all his faults recognised and respected the genius of his client and was willing to support him all the way.

Scumbag!! Asshole!!

And so Dylan and his band trooped out into the darkness of the stage.

Gary Stevens tries to introduce the ensemble, but already the sight of the band and the electric instruments has caused the crowd to escalate from booing to an animal howling. After a few moments tuning up Dylan and the group start off the second half with a spirited boogie version of 'Tombstone Blues.' The whistling and shouting which continues to rise, appears to climax by about the fourth line. Then the noise recedes for a moment. Maybe that's it? Maybe, having registered their displeasure, the audience is going to sit back and listen to what Dylan's got to offer?

Maybe, but the crowd had already been transformed from an audience of music fans to an angry mob, reeking of our animal origins. A mob runs on emotions, charged up with its own adrenaline, pumped to the gills with endorphins. You can't reason with a mob. And it was unlikely that the mob had suddenly seen sense.

'Tombstone Blues' finishes and the howling surges forward again. 'We want Dylan!' 'We want Dylan!' On the audiotape a voice near the microphone boos with a sound that turns into a yowling Neanderthal shriek. Then it abates again as Dylan and the band go into 'I Don't Believe You'.

At the end of every number the swelling sound rises again, the howling and the heckling, but it's perhaps at its most frightening when it surges upwards during 'Just Like Tom Thumb's Blues.' As Dylan finishes off the third line, the groaning rumble erupts once again and threatens to drown out the tune as it rolls around the stadium full of hatred and bile. At this point, a member of the crowd breaks through the security, and rushes the stage, knocking Al Kooper off his stool. Years later, when asked if things were then really getting out of hand, Kooper replied, 'No, it wasn't an outraged "folkie," it was just an obsessive fan.'

The mentality of the crowd and its schizophrenic fascism is captured on the third to last number, 'It Ain't Me Babe.' When the tune starts there are growls from the crowd. Then it goes silent until Dylan reaches the first line of the chorus, 'It ain't me babe,' then the growling once again bursts into howls of derision and shouts of 'No! No!' The mob calms down slightly, listens some more and then begin joining in on the choruses! Perhaps, we may allow ourselves the question, have they decided to enjoy themselves? But no. When 'It Ain't Me Babe' finishes, once again the tide of hatred surges forward threatening to drown out any onstage sound.

Dylan moves over to the piano for 'Ballad Of A Thin Man' and still standing, starts to play the opening riff. Still the yelling and persisting continued.

Al Kooper:'Dylan commanded us to "keep playing the intro over and over again until they shut up!" We played it for a good five minutes - doo do da da, do da de da - over and over until they did, in fact cool it.' At the end of the number the booing is noticeably less vociferous and the applause more genuine. This leads Dylan into what was to be the final number 'Like A Rolling Stone.'

From the audiotape it sounds like the same people who were booing earlier are now actually applauding the opening lines in recognition of the tune currently climbing up the charts. As it ends the applause from the audience is mixed. There's a lot of booing and some shouts for more. But

Dylan's thoughts are not on encores as he flees the stage, leaps straight into Kramer's car and hotfoots it back to Manhattan.

An interesting footnote from all this is that if you study Kramer's backstage photographs closely enough you can see that maybe, perhaps, and in spite of his apprehensions, Dylan hadn't anticipated it to be all gloom. There on the cue sheets is at least one encore number, 'Baby Let Me Follow You Down.' Clinton Heylin suggests that they might have rehearsed 'Highway 61' as well.

Oddly though, according to Al Kooper, Dylan enjoyed the show in spite of the booing. He relates in *Backstage Passes*, that back at Grossman's appartment that evening,

'Dylan bounded across the room and hugged us both. "It was fantastic," he said, "a real carnival and fantastic." He'd loved it.'

Although I cite Newport as the point of origin for Dylan and crew's strange journey into the unknown, the World Tour itself didn't begin in earnest until February 1966. The dates prior to that, and there are many, are points of consolidation and coalition, arenas of exchange where the new mercurial music was tested, as distinct from the later battle zones of full-scale confrontation.

The Ship She Is Sinking And I Am Afraid

Six days later, accompanied by the same crew, Dylan flew out to the West Coast and performed the same set in front of an LA audience at the Hollywood Bowl. This time things went differently. Whether the fans in LA were more hip to the changes that Dylan was going through, or had simply caught up with them, is a matter for conjecture. Whatever the case, Dylan was so pleased that he treated the audience to the encore that had been denied to the mob at Forest Hills.

Kooper and Brooks quit around mid-September. They had unwittingly plugged into a maelstrom of madness. They'd seen the face of the mob at its worst and they didn't like the hungry looks it had given them. To face that uncertainty every night, not knowing which way the crowd was going to go, playing on your wits and running for cover through crowded parking lots. Being called 'Asshole!' and 'Scumbag!' was too much for them. Life was a whole lot easier as session musicians.

Still, their departure gave Robbie Robertson the chance to be reunited with the rest of The Hawks and Dylan flew by private jet to Toronto on September 15 so he could begin rehearsals with them at a night-club called Friars the next day. Essentially this would be the unit for the world tour, although Hawks' drummer Levon Helm threw in the towel towards the end of November, unwilling to put up with the animosity generated by Dylan's new vision. Helm was replaced by Bobby Gregg who in turn would be replaced by Sandy Konikoff, before Mickey Jones settled into the drummer's hot seat in April 1966.

In his autobiography, *This Wheel's On Fire*, Helm documents the explanation he gave the rest of the band at the time:

'I said [that] "it was a ridiculous way to make a living: flying to concerts in Bob's 13-seat Lodestar, jumping in and out of limousines, and then getting booed... We'd never been booed in our lives... I can take getting booed here: this is my own country. But I can't see taking it to Europe and hearing this shit."'

During this final leg of 1965 when Dylan and The Hawks weren't touring they were in the studio working out the sound that in a 1978 *Playboy* interview, Dylan described like this -

'The closest I ever got to the sound I hear in my mind was on individual bands in the *Blonde On Blonde* album. It's that thin, that wild mercury sound. It's metallic and bright gold, with whatever that conjures up.'

In early October the ensemble had entered Columbia's Studio A in New York and cut three, possibly four tracks. 'Jet Pilot,' 'I Don't Wanna Be Your Partner I Wanna Be Your Lover,' a satirical riposte to The Beatles' 'I Wanna Be Your Man,' 'Medicine Sunday,' and crucially, the proposed follow up to 'Positively Fourth Street,' 'Can You Please Crawl Out Your Window.'

The Religion Of The Lilting Women

For a group who hadn't been playing together for even a month the recording of 'Can You Please Crawl Out Your Window' is quite remarkable and demonstrates the power and range that they'd later find together on stage. '...Window' is quite basically hatred you can dance to. But, bizarrely, hatred with a glockenspiel! Like a child's musical box with grinding electric guitar played like only Robertson could, smeared over the top. With its rinky dink cowbell percussion and words of spewed resentment - What the Hell was Dylan up to with this song?

With its direct reference to a male protagonist it has been the perceived wisdom to deconstruct this song along lover/jealousy lines. Perhaps as a plea to Sarah Lowndes who he was to marry on November 22, a month after the song was finished, perhaps as a putdown to one of his old Greenwich Village buddies? Or perhaps it's a commentary on the audiences that he and The Hawks had been encountering on their travels?

If the female in the song is Dylan's muse, or even his sensibility, then it makes an unusual sense to regard the masculine aspect of it as Dylan's vision of a Nemesis in the form of the archetypal Traditionalist; scowling, righteous and preoccupied with his vengeance for what is perceived as Dylan's selling out of Folk music. Dylan snarls, 'He looks so truthful, is this how he feels?' in reference to the implied purity of the Traditionalist. Dylan talks of how the male's 'Genocide fools and his friends rearrange their religion of the little ten women'.

When I first heard this song when it came out I thought Dylan sang - 'The religion of jilted women'. Then, after a while I began to hear it as - 'The religion of Lilting women' which is obviously much closer to a Folk traditional lyric, Lilting being a form of singing popularised on the West coast of Ireland and linked musicologically to Egyptian Keening, brought to Ireland in the 7th or 8th Century by Coptic missionaries. When *Writings And Drawings* was first published in 1973 and Dylan's 'official' lyrics were transcribed 'their religion of the little ten women' appeared and confusion grew from there.

Whatever the meaning of the 'little ten women', it appears that they back up the views of the male even though the face of the female is 'so bruised'. Although it is not made clear what she is bruised from. From the arguments over 'selling out,' commerciality, purism?

On The Road Again

The punishing schedule continued with gigs from Syracuse to California. By the time the band played Berkeley Community Theatre in December it must have seemed that things were levelling out. The audience was catching up to Dylan. However, memory can be a playful thing and as Greil Marcus notes in *Invisible Republic,* one man's past can be another woman's poison. What Greil had thought of for years as a moment of brightness within the tour, a moment when Dylan and his audience was simpatico, because Berkeley was beyond doubt seen as the hippest place in the universe, was cited by several other audience members from all those years ago as having been just as divisive just as chaotic and just as plain nasty as all the other gigs. One woman in particular saying that that was the time that Dylan turned his back on the people, literally and figuratively.

More gigs in late December and then it was New Year. Jesse Byron Dylan was born at the beginning of January and then it was back to business as usual. Most of the rest of the month was spent recording *Blonde On Blonde*, the name having been taken from a Clairol hair dye that used to be popular in the 1960s, whatever anyone else says.

More gigs followed, interspersed between sessions for the new album. In February the set list had coalesced into a solid, hard hitting, cold bladed strata of acoustic and electric that showed off the performer to his best advantage. That of being an artist at the cutting edge of creativity.

At White Plains 'Gates Of Eden' was replaced with 'Freeze Out,' the working title of 'Visions Of Johanna,' a song that was recorded with, amongst others, The Hawks for possible inclusion on *Blonde On Blonde*, but for the moment presented as an acoustic tune. The most urgent change at White Plains came with the electric set and the replacement of 'Tombstone Blues' as the opening number by 'Tell Me Momma.' 'Leopard Skin Pillbox Hat' replaces the Folk Rock version of 'It Ain't Me Babe.' February also saw the dropping of 'Positively Fourth Street' and the inclusion in the electric set of 'One Too Many Mornings.' To do this, with one of the songs off Dylan's most famously recognised 'Protest' album *The Times They Are A Changing*, can only be viewed as an act of direct provocation. Certainly in England it was seen as that by the die hard Traditionalists. Any vestige of integrity that Dylan possessed was destroyed when he wheeled out this Rock version of his past onto the stages of Australia and Europe. Was nothing sacrosanct?

During March, in between final sessions in Nashville for *Blonde On Blonde* the tour continued onwards, taking in Missouri, Nebraska, Denver, Wyoming, and then Vancouver before winding up in Tacoma. On April 9 Dylan and The Hawks climbed aboard an aeroplane and flew to Hawaii.

Laee'd In Hawaii

Bruce Cook in the Honolulu Advertiser set the tone for the rest of the World Tour:

'DYLAN EVENING A BIG LET-DOWN'

'He sings confusin' songs an he don't carry much of a tune (sic). Alone he can make more noise than The Beatles, Byrds and Animals put together. His followers are split into two factions - those who like him the way he used to be and those who like him now.'

Mr Cook continues:

'They call him a great poet, and some say he's a genius. But man, I say there's only one way to describe an evening with Bob Dylan: wasted.'

Cook went on to describe The Hawks as 'a run-of-the-mill rock group from Toronto.' He goes on to report 'the occasional cat-call or whistle and giggle'. He complains about the sound and finishes with an alleged quote from Dylan that he would one day be bigger than Elvis Presley (certainly a quote I've never seen anywhere), and finishes the review off with the following statement -

'Dylan and The Hawks left yesterday for a tour of Australia. It is said that someday he'll be bigger than Elvis Presley or The Beatles ever were. I can't believe that after watching his show.'

They Shot Ned Kelly Didn't They?

The following snippets are from the Sydney Airport press conference:

Are you a protest singer?

I haven't heard that word for a long time. Everybody knows there are no protest songs any longer. It's just songs.

Why have you gone commercial?

I have not gone commercial. I deny it (with bible swearing hand up-raised). Commercial - that's a word that describes old grandmothers that have no place to go.

Are you a professional beatnik?

Huh?

What's your real name?

William W. Kasanovarich.

Why did you change it?

Wouldn't you if you had a name like William W. Kasonovarich?

And so on and so on. The problem of course was that very few people got it.

Edgar Waters, writing for *The Australian* didn't get it:

'It was an ugly factory noise set to a factory rhythm, and Dylan's voice took on a new quality, as though he were shouting - though I suppose he was not actually shouting - to make himself heard above the mechanical din.'

The *Brisbane Daily Mail* hoped for 'an early death for folk-rock', and then it was on to Melbourne.

At Melbourne Airport it was another press conference and the same tired old round of banal queries -

How would you describe yourself?

I am a story-teller.

What is your greatest ambition?

To be a meat-cutter.

Can you enlarge on that?

Large pieces of meat.

Dylan played two nights in Melbourne at the Festival Hall. He and The Hawks met the same challenges that they had grown used to in America. Despite Dylan's voice obviously suffering from constant touring, the acoustic set went as well as it usually did, though the continuity was plagued by the seemingly endless amount of time that Dylan appeared to spend tuning up between numbers. The sets were coalesced now, laid down and didn't deviate from their standard pattern. Dylan and The Band were tight. They'd been playing too long with their backs up against the wall to let anything slip. It was the electric set that caused problems. The

sound as usual wasn't as good as it could have been. Tricia Jungwirth who was there remembers:

'It was so noisy (the music) that they (Dylan and The Band) couldn't be heard much .'

Sections of the audience heckled too -

'I remember more catcalls (than boos), people yelling insults... There were a lot of people who quite deliberately and conspicuously walked out as soon as the musicians walked onstage after intermission. Like they'd sat through the intermission so they could make this walk out protest thing. I'm pretty sure I can remember people holding up signs too. We thought it was pretty funny, being young teenagers who liked loud rock music and were glad Bob had "plugged in".'

We keep getting repeated references to the amount of time that Dylan spent tuning up (more of which later), and the 'stoned', or 'out of it' style of performance that he adopted at various gigs throughout the tour. This particular variation of the Dylan 'mystique' had been around for a long time. What was once described as 'Chaplinesque' by a variety of critics including luminaries such as Shelton, had, by 1965/66 become more problematical for the discerning writer, and probably for the average concert goer too.

At the start of Dylan's career, people had marvelled at how he managed to pull off the most amazing stunts on stage. Terri Van Ronk told Anthony Scaduto that -

'...He was onstage for forty minutes, and he kept falling off the stage... and it was so funny... and we all thought he was drunk. It took us a long time to figure out that when he fell off the stage it was timed, a planned thing, he was falling off within the context of the song, and it was hilarious.'

It seems Dylan was still capable of amazing people with his on-stage antics in 1966. Tricia Jungwirth remembers Melbourne -

'... Mostly all the "funny business" he did - the little Chaplin routines, a particularly long one with the piano stool just before the opening of "Ballad Of A Thin Man." It was one of those polished wooden stools and he pretended to slide off it underneath the piano, repeating the routine several times. I believe this was what led to the reports that he was so stoned he almost fell off the stage. I've never been able to reconcile how stoned he appeared with the absolutely spot-on timing of the comic turns, and the word perfect renditions of the songs.'

In Melbourne, Dylan took all of this to a completely new level. Coughing, tuning up, playing with lyrics - in 'Baby Let Me Follow You Down' 'Buy you a velvet shirt' becomes the wonderfully suggestive 'Buy you a gun that squirts'! His voice is rasping as if with tour fatigue, it had been a long haul. But, overall it sounds like a musician and a band that are actually having fun, Dylan playing out his little routines, deliberately creating the 'is he or isn't he?' mystique of the vagabond poet wild eyed and crazy, drunk on words or wine or both.

Unusually for Dylan he becomes very communicative with the audience during the acoustic set.

When he introduces 'Visions Of Johanna' he tells the assembled Melbourne cognoscenti that he's changed the title to 'Mother Revisited.' As he struggles to tune the guitar he explains -

'This isn't my guitar, that's why it keeps going out of tune all the time. My guitar got broken here in Australia and I had to borrow this one.... (he keeps struggling to get it in tune)... but it's a Folk music guitar.'

The crowd laugh, if a little nervously. The guy has just referred to their deepest fear, has Bob sold out? Would he prefer to be electric? What does he mean, it's a Folk music guitar?

Dylan saves his best for the second set with his introduction to 'Just Like Tom Thumb's Blues,' and he is unusually loquacious tonight (the full text of his rap is reprinted later). He even gets a teen scream from one of his fans.

Another Melbourne highlight was Dylan's performance of 'Just Like A Woman' - arguably one of the best of his career. It occupies a space that falls somewhere between languid and stoned. The guitar is a magic carpet ride travelling slowly over an empire created from Dylan's thoughts. The harmonica floats by on the clouds below. The vocal an incantation that guides us through the pain towards a bright light beyond.

Despite an astonishing, if at times a little ragged vocally, first half, and a sharper, grittier electric set than a lot of the European dates, Dylan still gets the slow hand-clapping, walkouts and boos that he and the rest of the crew have come to expect. The Traditionalists don't or won't get it. Oblivious to the power of Dylan's new vision, on point of principle, they refuse to let the music into their souls. Their hearts and ears are closed.

Back in the USA *Variety* ran a review of the concert under the headline-
BOB DYLAN DESTROYS HIS LEGEND IN MELBOURNE;
A few dates later the caravan embarked for Europe.

To Be Hip Or Not To Be Hip?... That Is The Hang Up.

The plane of fools touched down at Arlanda Airport in Sweden after a sleepless journey lasting 37 hours. A businessman disembarking from the same flight looked over his shoulder and shouted to the waiting Swedish press - 'Here come the animals!' It was not an auspicious start

The next day saw the usual round of press and radio interviews. The crushing inanity of the questions were guaranteed to rile Dylan who became, if such a thing was possible, even more obtuse than before.

Is it true that you give money to the US Civil Rights movement?

No, not true at all.

Do you have a message?

No. Do you?

What's your opinion of the Green Berets, the US Special Forces in Vietnam?

I was thinking of joining them. If they want me.

Several times during a radio interview with Klaus Burling Dylan tries to get Burling to understand where he's coming from. He tries so hard but Burling just doesn't get it:

KB: Should we try to listen to a song instead?

BD: We can try.

KB: Yeah? Which one would you suggest then?

BD: Uh, you pick one out, any one you say. You realise I'm not trying to be a bad fellow. I'm just trying to make it along and have a nice... get everything to be straight, you realise that?

KB:What would you call yourself, a poet or a singer, or do you think that you write poems and then you put music to it?

BD: No... I don't know... It's so silly I mean, you can't... You wouldn't ask those questions of a carpenter, would you? Or a plumber?

On 29 April Dylan and The Band played at the Stockholm Konserthus to a capacity audience, and the next day made the short trip to Copenhagen. The inevitable press conference followed, this time however, an unnamed journalist from the Danish communist paper *Land og Folk* did understand:

'Having held many press conferences, Bob Dylan has learned that most of the journalists who turn up don't know the slightest thing about his music, his art, and that consequently meaningful dialogue with them is impossible. The questions directed at him are usually pointless. "What do you think of Danish girls? Where are you going after this concert? Where have you just come from, and how was it there?"... Dylan's parody of a press conference was perfect, but the journalists were furious at the end of it all. "Who does he think he is?" some of them muttered.'

Later that day the entourage, now accompanied by D.A. Pennebaker's film crew, set off to visit Hamlet's castle at Kronberg. Free from tour hassles for a while, Dylan seemed more relaxed and contemplative. While

Grossman, in flat cap and tweed jacket, looked every inch a country squire. Pennebaker, meanwhile, sported a grey top hat as he stalked Dylan with his camera. Dylan and Richard Manuel tried to buy a blonde Scandinavian girl but her boyfriend wouldn't take Australian dollars. Later they all returned to Copenhagen, where the next night Dylan played the KB-Hallen concert Hall. The following afternoon Dylan left Scandinavia for London.

England Swings

Dylan's English work permit, number 700935, described him as a 'Variety Artiste', which is a fairly accurate description of how the tabloid newspapers treated him at the inevitable press conference at the Mayfair Hotel on May 3rd.

Why don't you write protest songs anymore?

All my songs are protest songs. You name something, I'll protest about it.

Why do some of your songs bear no relation to the titles?

Give me an example.

'Rainy Day Women No's 12 and 35.'

Have you ever been in North Mexico?

The next day Paul McCartney visited Dylan at the Mayfair and played him the new Beatles' album, *Revolver*. Dylan reciprocated by playing him acetates of *Blonde On Blonde*. Unfortunately, there is nothing on record about McCartney's reaction to the 'Norwegian Wood' parody/tribute 'Fourth Time Around.' Lennon, the main author of 'Norwegian Wood' however had made no secret of his admiration for Dylan at the time of writing *Rubber Soul*, and after hearing 'Fourth Time Around' was reported as feeling 'paranoid' at Bob's apparent dig at his expense.

On Erin's Fair Shore

Before playing in Britain, Dylan had to perform two concerts in Ireland, Dublin and Belfast. Dublin is where the storm broke.

DUBLIN: NIGHT OF THE BIG LETDOWN.

POP GOES BOB DYLAN - AND 'BOO' GO FANS.

FANS SHOCKED BY BOB DYLAN.

DYLAN: THE FALLEN IDOL.

The above are just a selection of the reviews following the gig at the Adelphi Theatre. Since first hearing of him the Irish had held him as one of their own, a prophet in the Bardic firmament. Ireland, more than anywhere else perhaps, was steeped in a living Folk tradition. Dylan had lent credence to something that was perceived as being old fashioned or out dated, even embarrassing. Why, wasn't he the best of friends with Tommy Maken and The Clancy Brothers? Hadn't he single handedly dragged Folk out of the clutches of whimsy and dragged it to the forefront of social comment? And now the feckin eedjit was about to ruin it all with his electric guitars and Rock 'n' Roll!

By all accounts the second half of the Dublin concert became a battleground. Robbie Robertson claims he can remember seeing people holding placards saying 'Stop The War!'! Shrieks and taunts split the air as audience members vied with one another to shout the most derisive insult.

'Leave it to The Beatles!'

'Positively BORE Street!'

'Stuffed golliwog!'

'Lower the mike!'

'Throw out the backing group!'

All of the above taunts took place amidst a wall of slow hand-clapping and booing.

The newspaper reviews were almost as bad.

'The barrage of amplification equipment completely drowned Dylan's nasal voice, which requires the utmost concentration at the best of times.

'His beat arrangements were monotonous and painful, as folk useless and as beat, inferior. "Like A Rolling Stone" had some merit.

'There were a few diehards who clapped until the end. They'll never learn.'

So wrote Norman Barry in the *Irish Sunday Independent*.

There is one track out on official release from this concert, 'I Don't Believe You.' It came out on *Biograph* where it was incorrectly attributed to Belfast, which Dylan played on the following night.

And Arrived On England's Green and Pleasant Shores

On May 10, Dylan played at Bristol Colston Hall and got the following review in the Western Daily Press:

'Bob Dylan, the folk-singer prophet of the modern generation, parted company with many of his fans at the Colston Hall, Bristol, this week. His long awaited second appearance in the city turned out to be a noisy, blaring, ear-splitting disaster.'

When you listen to the tape of the Bristol gig, with the exception of an unbelievably astonishing harmonica solo in 'Mr Tambourine Man,' the acoustic set sounds tired. Dylan fluffs lines and works hard to push some enthusiasm into his singing. He has trouble reaching notes and on occasions during 'Baby Blue' doesn't even bother trying. The electric set though is dynamic and enthusiastic, even if the audience is less so. After the usual opening number of 'Tell Me Momma' there is polite, tentative applause. When that's died down and everybody's waiting for the next number a voice shouts, 'Will you turn the volume down please?' A ludicrous, polite English voice. None of your Irish screaming, here is the voice of reason, gently pointing out to Bob the error of his ways. Dylan replies with a query, 'You don't like rock 'n' roll?' and then proceeds to blast into 'I Don't Believe You,' a suitably apt title.

To be fair, just before the final number another voice roars out of the crowd - '"Rolling Stone" Bob! Come on! "Rolling Stone!"' But set amongst the booers and those who walked out it's a shame there weren't more to shout in defence of Dylan.

'Angry of Bristol, Cardiff, Leicester, Liverpool and Sheffield'

Here's a letter from the following week's *Melody Maker* -

'I have just attended a funeral at Bristol's Colston Hall. They buried Bob Dylan, the folk-singer, in a grave of electric guitars, enormous speakers and deafening drums. It was a sad end to one of the most phenomenal influences in music. My only consolation is that Woody Guthrie wasn't there to witness it.

Jenny Leigh, Bristol.'

And here's another -

'I have just come back from a concert which was the most ridiculous load of tripe I've ever seen. The first half was superb with Dylan singing and playing in his natural way. Then came the Group, making Dylan's singing inaudible and the songs absolutely meaningless. Dylan has just lost two fans (me and my boyfriend).

Miss L. Cutler, Upper Gornal,

Let us pause briefly to decode the content of these two letters, because they reflect deeply the response towards Dylan on the whole of the world tour. The basic charge laid by the Traditionalists against Dylan is that of 'traitor'. Treacherous against what in particular isn't made specific, but is implied by the inclusion of keywords such as 'Folk-singer,' 'Woody Guthrie,' and 'natural'. 'Natural' is the most emotionally laden word here. It's a signifier adrift in a sea of hurt. For Dylan to sing unaccompanied is 'natural'. Would he be therefore even more 'natural' if he didn't even use a guitar? For Jenny Leigh it was the electric guitars that caused so much pain; the 'folk-singer' had 'died', and was duly buried under the equipment. It would be far too easy for me to make much more of this, especially with the benefit of hindsight, so I leave it to another letter writer to the *Melody Maker*, Erica Davies, who attended the show on the following night in Cardiff.

'I would like to protest against the attitude of some of Dylan's audiences. To shout 'traitor' and walk out because he appeared with an electric guitar was puerile. These people must have been walking round with their ears plugged as Dylan's last two LPs and seven singles have all featured electric guitars, and it was well known in advance he was bringing a backing group with him.'

What Ms Davies says here is so obvious, it makes one wonder why Ms Leigh and Ms Cutler didn't get it. But, maybe we have to bear in mind the concept of wish fulfilment: 'I wish he hadn't 'sold out', therefore I'll go to his concert and it'll be alright'. Tricia Jungwirth has argued that there was some kind of 'collective amnesia' in operation. Had people 'conveniently' forgotten the recordings of the previous year? But the principal question is, why should they want to? Is it because they'd found something within the world of 'Folk' that represented to them a better, more decent approach to culture and society than they had been used too? Was Folk intrinsically linked to better values and higher morals? Possibly so, at least for them, but what such analysis leads to is restating the almost messianic

position that Dylan held for a large proportion of his fans. He was the Folk prophet - or whatever you wanted him to be. He had moved on - it was up to them to follow him or go another way.

Maybe it was his very exclusivity of style that had attracted them to him. Dylan, the 'Folk poet' was a romantic, isolated figure, described by one Jon Holliday in *Melody Maker* again, as - '... this young genius poet, ragamuffin minstrel, the American Yevtushenko, Jimmie Dean with a guitar, beatnik bard, the hippies' Homer, the Great Protester.' And when Dylan had the unmitigated audacity to appear on stage with other musicians, just like any other Beat Group - Mr. Holliday continues - 'he became just another beat group singer, hollering, gyrating, gesticulating, mouthing, indistinguishable from the countless grains of sand on the beach called Merseyside.'

At Birmingham on May 12, members of the audience shouted that they wanted 'Some Folk music!' Barely able to supress his rage Dylan answered them with this -

'If you want some Folk music, I'll play you some Folk music... This is a Folksong my grandaddy used to play for me... He used to take me on his knee and he used to sing this song for me ... It goes like this ...'

Dylan and the band then launched into a hard rocking version of 'Baby Let Me Follow You Down.'

Warfare all the way.

At Birmingham they walked out screaming 'Get the group off!'

The reporter from the student newspaper *Redbrick* claimed that Dylan had 'sold his soul'. The audience cried out that he was 'A Folk phony', and 'We want Folk!'

On May 14, Liverpool and the home (nominally) of The Beatles, one of the audience shouted - 'Where's the poet in you?!?' and 'Where's your conscience?!?'

Dylan admirably replied - 'There's a guy up there looking for a saint.'

May 15, and more of the same, aside from the belligerently Northern accent that cries out - 'Rock it Bob! You're the greatest!'

Robbie Robertson told Barney Hoskyns that at one venue on the tour:

'People actually attacked the stage. People had things like scissors in their hands, it was quite frightening. Man, you were thinking in terms of instruments as weapons, that you were going to have to knock some-body's head off.'

The momentum continued on May 16, at the Gaumont Theatre in Shef-field.

'Traitor!' - 'Play Folk songs!' - Go and play with the Rolling Stones!' - And perhaps, most cutting of all - 'We don't need you!'

The next day, the entourage set off across the Pennines for Manchester.

CHAPTER FIVE
The Geography Of Innocence

Rainsoaked, raw and cleft atwixt two rivers, the first Mancunians took shelter from the elements and their enemies on the sandstone ground that gave the village its name - Manchun, the Brigante for Red Rock. Not long after, the Romans came and brought with them their roads, their laws and their gods. High upon the garrison wall Centurion Marcus Longinius pauses long enough to wrap his damp woollen cloak closer round his body and accidentally drops a coin that falls to the ground, which then lies there for nearly two thousand years covered by successive layers of muck, dust and filth. Until one day, in the late 20th century, it would be dug up by an archaeologist called Diane, and put on show for schoolchildren.

A Quick Trip Through Time

During the Middle Ages a cathedral was built at the far end of Deansgate, or, the Street of Danes, a sign of a turbulent past. Long ships full of marauding Vikings burning and looting. Fear ran deep in the soul and the city was defended. Just south of the old city a great scar was hacked into the ground, an 'earthwork', a barricade, a long lazy trench called the Nico. Fragments are still there, long straight lines, abandoned long ago and defaced by age, but you can stand by the side of them and close your eyes and dream a Saxon dream. Strange to think of that other Nico, the chanteuse from the Velvet Underground, for whom Dylan wrote 'I'll Keep It With Mine' and who would spend her sad final years in Manchester.

A Quicker Trip

The settlement had grown into a modestly sized town by the time of Elizabeth 1st, the Virgin Queen, and unwitting servitor of the Rosicrucian enlightenment. She sent to Manchester her Court Astrologer, the Magickian and Philosopher, Doctor John Dee to take control of Chetham's Grammar School in 1589, thereby initiating a centuries old Hermetical Magick tradition that persists to this day. Here in the mist shrouded streets of the old town he is said to have perfected the vocabulary of the language of Angels, or Enochian, by which he allegedly obtained conversation with those spirits and entities that dwell in realms beyond our own.

Among the spirits he conversed with was Mercury.

And Even Quicker

Machines and choking smoke made modern Manchester. Raging furnaces and clattering shuttles. Goods and people were sucked into the vacuum out of which spewed the products of commerce and industry. And in Manchester, as with all Northern Industrial cities in that era, unspeakable misery and suffering lived cheek by jowl with magnificent opulence.

Just off Albert Square, site of the Victorian town hall, is Brasenose Street, where you can find a statue of Abraham Lincoln, sent to the good people of Manchester by a grateful Union after the close of the Civil War. Even though they were starving as a result of the Northern blockade of Confederate ports, the cotton workers of Manchester marched in their thousands to defy segregation and slavery.

How Much Faster Can We Go?

By 1966, the city and its people had endured the Romans, the Danes, the Normans, typhoid, cholera, bubonic plague, the Industrial Revolution, the Great War, the Depression, the Nazi firestorms of the Second World War, and now they wanted to party.

In 1966 Manchester was at war with its young people. In 1965 the City Fathers and the Chief of Police had bamboozled the House of Commons into passing a special Act of Parliament that effectively banned Beat Clubs from operating within the city. Going into operation from January 1st 1966, this Draconian piece of legislation was the harbinger of doom for this hideaway, hedonist lifestyle of a generation. One by one the clubs fell foul of the intricacies of the new law, and one by one they were closed down with nary a protest or a by your leave. Being a kid wasn't fun anymore. The cops kicked in a curfew designed to prevent people under eighteen from being out on the street after 10.30. If you were found in a club, you were busted - end of argument - and you'd go to jail where your parents were called to come and pick you up. From nearly 200 clubs in the Greater Manchester area in the early 1960s, by the time Bob Dylan came a calling there were barely a handful.

Going to the Free Trade Hall wasn't regarded as a potentially criminal activity however. In fact, going to the Free Trade Hall was quite 'posh'. It was a grown-up thing. A proper concert - a special occasion. You could even buy souvenir programmes.

More History

It had been built in the 19th century on the site of the Peterloo Massacre, when an unarmed crowd of pro-democracy supporters were charged by mounted militia. At the end of the day nineteen lay dead and hundreds were injured. The people of Manchester wanted a functional memorial to the fallen, and the Free Trade Hall was born. Over the years it hosted everything from circuses to political rallies, Classical music concerts to boxing matches. It really was a hall for everyone. The inside was gutted by fire during the Christmas Blitz of 1941, but rebuilt on an even grander scale during the post-war reconstruction. In the 1960s there was an event on there nearly every night and Bob Dylan had already played there in 1965.

1966 was a strange time in Manchester. It was a transition point from the spirit of the 1950s towards something else. Something that was monumentally awesome. Only we didn't know it at the time. If you check out photos and film footage from the period you can sense that there's a change in the air, but just like the photographs, the moment is frozen. It hasn't moved on yet.

The reality of living in a provincial town was significantly different from the images of 'Swinging' London and the Poptastic world of Carnaby Street, Modesty Blaise and David Bailey, that loomed out at us from the (newly created) Sunday Newspapers' colour supplements.

The 'neo-culture' and counter culture were in embryonic flux. We were aware of poets and writers like Ginsberg and Burroughs, often chiefly through the influence of Dylan in my case. The existence of 'Underground' movies, music, magazines and papers, were trickling into our consciousness via word of mouth and reports in the 'hipper' columns of the standard music journals, but these were very early days. Nobody had any idea of what a 'hippy' was, let alone becoming one. Of all the standard bearers Dylan was the primary signifier of the changes about to be wrought. Some, like the old time Beats who had been there to see him in 65, were talking of the times a coming, but basically we were still operating within the confines of a 19th century consensus. You went to school, you left school and you got a job. The only difference in 1966 was that more of us were being programmed to go to university or college (if we weren't there already).

Modern Times/Hard Times

For two people in particular, the 17th May 1966, may as well have been 1866. Clifford Coop of Atherton, just outside Manchester was sent to jail for four months for stealing 11 shillings (55 pence) from a gas meter. Meanwhile, in Stockport, Hilda Cousins was remanded in custody in Risley Prison for three weeks, while investigations continued over the alleged theft of a leg of lamb worth 12/6d (work it out for yourself) from newly opened supermarket, Tescos.

Reading through contemporary news reports for the time that Dylan and crew visited Manchester, one could be forgiven for occasionally thinking that you'd slipped back into the past. Footpads and ne'er do wells inhabited the highways and byways. Although there don't seem to have been any more or any less murders than there are now in the 1990s. The usual tragic crop of 'killed in an argument over the price of a fish supper'. 'Was drunk when argument started'. All the sad, tired, old reasons that have come out for century after century. Myra Hindley, one of the convicted

'Moors' Murderers' serial killers, was appealing against her sentence of life imprisonment, and still is, as of this book being written in 1998.

At the cinema inklings of a new way of seeing things were percolating through to the local flea pits. *Georgy Girl*, in which Lynne Redgrave turned from being a frumpy dance teacher into a swinging 60's chick. *Cul-de-Sac*, one of Roman Polanski's last European movies before moving to Hollywood and falling foul of the Manson Family. Truffaut's *Fahrenheit 451* wove nightmares around the idea of a world filled with intolerance. And Peter Brook's *Marat Sade* brought an intellectual seal of approval to Artaud's concepts of the Theatre of Cruelty. How shamefully the latter two movies would link Dylan's tour with the cinematic mirror that cultural critics claim is held up to society is a matter of conjecture, but Brook and Artaud have both been held up to ridicule by their own particular provenances, Dylan by his.

We've Gotta Get Out Of This Place

Trying to escape the cloying confines of an industrial, provincial city was more difficult than it would seem to someone from this end of the 20th century. Very few people owned cars, trains and coaches were expensive, irregular and inconvenient. Movement was hard, or static. It was stated ironically that there were only two ways out of Manchester - the M62 motorway, or the bottle. But there were other ways too, university or the army, and most of us in the 1960s were groomed one way or the other from early childhood to accept the route that fate had dictated. That's why Dylan was so important to many of the people who went to see him that night. He represented an alternative escape route that defied the dictates of society. It was an escape route that existed through the liberation of one's own head.

It Must Be True, I Seen It On TV

The cerebral delights of English television wouldn't have been much good at aiding attempts at emancipation either. Although an 'alternative', intellectual channel, BBC 2, had just come on air, the proto-freaks and neo-hippies would find little on air to carry them out of the crushing mundanity of everyday existence. US import 'Hiram Holliday' was a moderate diversion at teatime on the day of Dylan's gig. That was on BBC 1. Over on Granada, Chuck Connors in 'The Rifleman' led the evening schedules boldly forward until at 7pm, when Hughie Green, 'Mr. TV,' invited punters to 'Double Your Money'. An eerie forerunner of 'ER' - 'Emergency Ward Ten' followed, and a feature film dominated the rest of the evening until, at 10-35, another US import, 'The Untouchables', brought the evening to a close at the frighteningly late hour of 11-30pm.

Meanwhile, BBC 1, had reached its close down at 11-15pm after an evening of unmitigated boredom, the highlight of which was 'Bonjour Francois', a French primer for nouveau holiday makers. Over on BBC 2, the tone of the evening's viewing was set with the first programme of the day - 'Advances In Language Teaching', which came on air at 7.30pm. As a concession to the modern age, and just to show how hip the BBC was, its late night arts show, 'Late Night Line Up', went on air at 11-10 and very often didn't finish until midnight! To be fair, it was a show that was often controversial and lively. Several years later they did day by day coverage of the Chicago Conspiracy Trial, but in 1966 they either hadn't heard of Dylan, or the budget didn't stretch to including him on the BBC's premier arts flagship.

Dylan might not have been on television that Tuesday night, but he was in *The Manchester Evening News*, placed above the TV listings. The piece was written by James Fox and headed - THE ARTIST WHO'S JUST A BIG MYSTERY. A standard record company photograph dating back at least a year was featured prominently on the top right hand corner of the page.

Fox writes a reasonably sympathetic piece about Dylan, his relationship with the press, how his songs speak for him, and the controversy over his use of backing musicians.

'Now there is something disturbing about Dylan; he is said to have disowned all the songs he ever wrote before he turned to "folk-rock". He is said to have become an introvert. He was nearly booed off the stage in Dublin recently when he came on with three tons of sound equipment and his new backing group - simply called the Group!'

Fox finishes off the article by stating that tonight at the Free Trade Hall we will get our chance to see whether Dylan has turned his back on us. Indeed we would.

The Night Comes Falling.

So there we were, that mild, early spring day, getting ready to see Bob Dylan. 1800 people from all over the city, gearing up to see the poet, each with their own expectations of what the night would bring.

Dave Rothwell was a young catering student at Hollins College. What had brought him there that night?

'I used to go out with a girl who liked Traditional Folk music; she was of Belfast origins. The McPeake Family, the Clancy Brothers, that sort of thing. We used to go to the Pack Horse Folk club on Bridge Street. One night a guy got up and sang "The Lonesome Death Of Hattie Carroll"... I thought it was a marvellous song and I tried to find out who did it. Somebody said it was the bloke who wrote "Blowin' In The Wind." That was in 1964.'

Malcolm Metcalfe -

'I come from a very working class background in Salford, and I was 16 when The Beatles were first around. Pop music took over our lives basically. Everybody was looking for something and I know I certainly was. The Beatles, The Stones, I saw them all live and they all meant a hell of a lot to us in those times. I guess I heard of Dylan through John Lennon. He started spouting about somebody called Dylan, who I'd never heard of. I remember being 17 and my father had remarried which upset me quite a lot. I remember being fairly confused and Lennon was going on about Dylan. I was getting a bit fed up with Pop music. I went out one day and thinking I wanted a bit of a change, I went into a record shop and bought a Georgie Fame album and *Another Side Of Bob Dylan.* ... Georgie Fame didn't particularly turn me on... But the Dylan thing from that moment on basically took over my life. Dylan completely changed my life. No doubt about it.'

Over thirty years later, Malcolm told me how -

'It was just Dylan. The lyrics, the whole thing of Dylan. What it did turn me onto, interestingly enough, was poetry. I mean, there I was, a working class kid, secondary modern school background, I wanted to find out more about Dylan. He was talking about the French Symbolist poets. He was into Blues.... [so] I bought Robert Johnson albums and stuff like that. But it was the poetry that I got into more... He led me to literature, in a very intense way.... This started a kind of odyssey for me and I started wandering.... When I was 22 I found out about this Adult Education College... I did a two-year course, and then the academic life took over.... Like I say, Dylan totally changed my life...''

Tim and Kath Green were typical Mancunian Mod teenagers -

'I was a machine operator in a paper mill. Kath was still a schoolgirl. I spent all my money on clothes and records as was befitting at the time. That was my life at the time - clothes and music. We first heard Dylan through Radio Caroline (a pirate radio station), or something like that.'

Stewart Tray first heard Dylan in 1964 -

'I think the first song I heard was "Blowin' In The Wind". I was at school at the time and first heard it through a friend of mine. I didn't have a record player at home, and this friend said "listen to this album".'

It's hard now as we hurtle towards the end of the 20th century to imagine a time when a record player was regarded as a luxury item. Steve Currie, who was also a schoolboy back then, recalled -

'We didn't have a record player. I used to have to go round to friends' houses to listen to Dylan.'

Several of the concert goers I interviewed couldn't afford to buy copies of *The Times They Are A Changing* until 1966, over two years after it had been released. This was a period in time where to own a 45-rpm single was a major investment; an album was a prized object of desire equal to its weight in gold. For Stewart, his friends' record players opened up a Pandora's box of possibilities.

'I'd never heard anything like Dylan. All we were listening to was The Beatles and The Stones like everyone else at the time. But this was something that I'd never heard before, speaking sense in songs. All we'd ever had before was "I love you, you love me"... These songs were quite astonishing.'

Another friend told Paul Kelly that he should listen to Dylan. So he went out and bought a copy of *Freewheeling*.

'I decided I wanted to play a bit of guitar. I got a guitar for Christmas and that was the time that I started listening to Dylan because his stuff was accessible. You could listen to it and play it.'

Like many of us the album covers particularly struck him.

'... The cover of *Freewheeling* - every young boy's fantasy of walking around with this beautiful young woman on your arm, and you didn't have to be rich and all the rest of it.'

The cover of *Highway 61* provided the basis for a conspiracy to infiltrate Dylan and his entourage at the Midland Hotel on the night of the gig.

'We used to hang out in the Cona Coffee Bar on Tib Street, an existentialist coffee bar all painted black. I can remember one particular evening in there just before the gig. We decided that we could blag our way into the Midland to see Dylan by pretending to be the members of his backing band. We picked the names off the back of the album. Who was going to be Mike Bloomfield, etc. I wound up as Charlie McCoy. We had no idea that the musicians would be different. It never occurred to us.'

After the gig, Paul and his friends went round to the back of the Free Trade Hall hoping to catch a glimpse of Dylan (as did many others), but he'd already gone. So they set off, high on the energy of the gig, laughing and jabbering, around the corner to the hotel. After standing around on the steps for a while, common sense overcame them and they abandoned the idea of the masquerade and, instead, went off home. Which, in a way, is a bit of a shame. The sight of five Salford schoolboys trying to pass themselves off as a group of America's top session players would have been a sight to behold.

Dave Rothwell, like myself, had come into it via Folk music:

'My girlfriend and her family used to sing songs at home around the fire. Slowly I got to like it so much that I got a guitar and learned how to play it. At college I ran the Folk club for a couple of years. I come from Wythenshawe and there wasn't really anybody else in that area who was into Folk, though I do remember one night in a fish and chip shop I got cornered by a psycho who said to me - "Which one are you into... Dylan or Donovan?"'

The wrong answer could potentially have led to a beating up. After some careful consideration Dave answered 'Dylan.' The maniac shook his hand and walked off into the night to stalk easier prey.

Roger and Jane Harvey found themselves at the Free Trade Hall because they attended all sorts of concerts there. They were mainly into Jazz and Blues but had heard about Dylan and thought that a visit might be worthwhile.

'We were on the mailing list. We'd been to see people like The Spinners (an English Folk group) and Joan Baez. When we saw that Dylan was on, we thought, why not?'

And Darkness Is All Around.

In comparison to today's mega-media hypes and attendant publicity campaigns with radio, press and TV tie-ins, once again it's hard to imagine what it was like in the mid 1960s. The promotion for Dylan's gig was exactly as it had been the year before. One advert in *The Manchester Evening News* and a hand-written sign in the window of a record store on Peter Street called Hime and Addison, where the tickets were on sale. Publicity at that stage was still very much a word of mouth thing. Today, attendance at Dylan concerts is facilitated through the Internet. People travel to every gig that they can get to, often planning their vacations around them. Back in those days the very idea was unthinkable. You went to the gig in your own hometown. Why on earth would I have gone across the Pennines to Sheffield or down the East Lancs Road to Liverpool to see other Dylan concerts? It was just totally unfeasible, economically and statistically. Very few of us had phones let alone, cars. Trains and coaches were prohibitive, not to mention the price of tickets when you got there.

The Price Of Admission Is Your Soul!

My ticket for the Free Trade Hall cost 12 shillings and 6 pence (about 65 new pence). On the night of the concert I had enough for my bus fare there and back, and just enough for a soft drink. I didn't even have 2s and 6d for a programme. No, the idea of going to gigs in other towns was strictly no-go in the 1960s.

Malcolm Metcalfe had been on the road when he came back to Manchester that week and found out that Dylan was on -

'I remember coming home and finding out that Dylan was on at the Free Trade Hall and going there and being really surprised that I couldn't get a ticket. I couldn't get in! I just thought, "Oh, I'll just go there and get in!"'

Dave Rothwell had taken the day off college to buy his tickets.

Kevin Fletcher, a junior technician at Manchester University had bought five for himself and his friends at Hime and Addison, the week before.

Stewart Trey knew a girl in his street who worked at the ticket outlet. He knew precisely where he wanted to sit -

'I said to her, there's a rumour that Dylan's going to play in Manchester. If he does I want three tickets. She said no problem where do you want to sit? I said I'd like to sit where I sat for the Joan Baez concert - platform tickets - on the stage.'

Platform tickets were an interesting concept that appears to have fallen out of favour these days. In order to cram more people in and therefore make more money, promoters had noticed that a lot of these performers were either solo or unencumbered with masses of equipment, so why not, they reasoned, put seats on the stage? The fact that a whole lot of people throughout the heady days of the sixties only ever managed to see the backs of performer's heads was by the by. Hopefully artists would occasionally turn round at the end of a number to take a bow, thereby granting the lucky few a momentary intimacy denied to those in the stalls and balcony. Stewart got his three platform tickets. You can see him and his friends on the photographs accompanying this book.

Tim Green got his tickets from a department store called Lewis's -

'At the time Lewis's in Manchester had a booking office upstairs, right on the top floor, and 'cos I got paid on Thursdays, I went every Thursday from when I heard that he was going to be on in Manchester, trying to get tickets. And the lady kept saying "No, we don't know anything about it." Eventually, I got the tickets!'

Paul Kelly:

'As soon as the dates of the tour were known it was tapping money off the old lady and into town. I got my tickets at Hime and Addison, down in the basement. The ticket cost 20 shillings. There were four or five of us.'

A Moment Of Nostalgia In A Record Store

The basement of the erstwhile record store-come-ticket shop had become something of a Mecca for young Dylan fans. On the wall Mr Hime, or Mr Addison, we'll never know for sure, had pinned up two icons of exquisite delight to the aficionados of the minstrel poet. One was a French poster for who knows what, showing Dylan holding a Fender bass guitar. This was big. The second item was the sleeve for a French or Dutch release of 'Mixed Up Confusion,' featuring the same picture, but this time - smaller! Enquiries as to the availability of the aforementioned recording always met with charming but evasive answers from the girls who worked behind the counter. 'No' they hadn't heard of the record. There might have been a record to go with the sleeve, but 'no, sorry, we're not allowed to sell it'. This tactical evasion went on for at least three years when the poster and sleeve mysteriously disappeared. I can remember one time being told that they weren't available because it was illegal to sell imports without a licence. When pressed about why they had the sleeve on display they would revert to the 'I'm sorry, I don't know anything about it' mode.

Far Out - On A Learning Curve

It was hard to contain my excitement at school on the 17th May. There were only two of us from there going, Mike King and myself, but we made sure everybody else knew about it.

Wh'appen when you were flung around in the maelstrom that was the mid-sixties? Whether you lived in England, Scandanavia, Australia or the United States, Dylan was, perhaps, the only barometer that you possessed, even if he cried out, in a voice so redolent of prophecy - 'You don't need a weatherman to know which way the wind blows' - that wasn't sufficient. We needed to know more. Malcolm, Paul, Kath, Barbara, Tricia, Tim, myself and a hundred thousand others looked to Dylan for a signal, a sign. He gave it, of course, but I doubt whether any of us there was able to receive the message personally, as it were - Dylan was too far ahead of anybody in a two bit town in the North West of England, for us to be able to comprehend fully, though we all did our hardest to try it.

The problem was, we took along all the cultural baggage that we had already been saddled with. The thousands of years of Judeo-Christian programming that stifled and moulded our minds. Whether we were Irish second generation immigrants, students only here for three years, or children of the damp soil of the Rainy City, we were rooted too deeply in the earth of Manchester to be able to grasp the full significance of Dylan's credo - 'Think for yourself'. Here was a poet, a prophet, who almost came from the same roots as us.

Oh, yes, we knew Bob wasn't so different. Deep down inside. If he came from Hibbing there was a relationship with the North - South - East - West of England, name your space, because he was from us. Whatever Dylan was singing about had a resonance that reverberated throughout us all. You could have been a coal miner, a clerk, a secretary, a hotel-maid. Maybe, you could even have been a president. Sooner or later Dylan would have spoken directly to you - at least that's what we believed. (And maybe still do). Just because he was from Hibbing/Duluth/New York, or wherever, made no difference at all. Dylan spoke with a voice that echoed our thoughts, spoken or unspoken. He articulated the desires of a generation. And tonight, tonight in Manchester, for all of us, he was going to be there.

CHAPTER SIX
Mr Tambourine Man

A Little Local Difficulty

Meanwhile, inside the Free Trade Hall, all was not well.

The management had anticipated a simple affair like the previous year's performance - one man, one microphone. They were horrified when, just before 2pm, a large articulated lorry pulled up at the back entrance on Windmill Street and two gruff looking Americans stepped down from the van and approached them.

'Is this the way we take the equipment?'

The assembled porters and cleaners looked on in horror as the back of the truck began to disgorge its load of gear. Taken completely by surprise they had no alternative but to help the American road crew with moving the load down the narrow backstage corridors and onto the stage.

A further shock greeted 'AS', the manager of the Free Trade Hall, when Fred Perry, the Columbia UK representative, arrived just moments later and informed him that the concert was going to be recorded and where could the engineers put their equipment?

A London firm, IBC, had been hired to record at least four of the English shows for possible consideration as a 'live' album release. Columbia had quite diligently been recording Dylan at a variety of venues from as far back as his 1963 New York Town Hall gig. The Columbia Art Department even have a fully mocked up sleeve for 'Bob Dylan In Concert', dating back to 1964.

While 'AS' was grappling to let the news sink in, further disruption was caused by the arrival of DA Pennebaker's film crew. When Howard Alk's wife, Jones, who was in charge of recording the film sound, asked where she and Robert Van Dyke could set up their Nagra recording equipment, disbelief had set in.

Now the manager of the Free Trade Hall, the most prestigious municipal building in Manchester, was getting totally phased. It had gone two in the afternoon, Bob Dylan was due to arrive for a soundcheck at four o'clock, and his stage area was crawling with aliens from the planet Mindgon, pulling down the platform seats to make way for a mountain of speakers and a drum riser.

He did what any self respecting servant of the City Council would do under the circumstances and took to his office at the top of the building and began making telephone calls to the promoter of tonight's concert, Tito Burns. We know how irate he was from a letter sent to Tito's office the next day -

'You will recall that phone calls to your office yesterday obtained your agreement to the recording by C.B.S. Recordings of the Bob Dylan concert held at the Free Trade Hall last evening. You will also be aware that the conditions of letting permit recordings to be taken provided that the written consent of the Manager (myself) is given and that the hirer must inform me in writing not less than 21 days beforehand of such intentions to record.'

(underlining in original)

I may do 'AS' a disservice by presenting him as a 'jobsworth'. This was the first time a Rock band had played at the venue. Presumably all other live recordings done there had been arranged through the proper channels. The Halle Orchestra broadcasted regularly from the Free Trade Hall. Jazz concerts had been recorded there and because these occurrences were so regular a multi-directional microphone was permanently suspended midway over the stalls to pick up the applause. The microphone was fed into a cubbyhole sized room at the side of stage left, just past the wings. BBC audio engineers, or whoever, would crouch in there as a kind of makeshift outside broadcast/recording studio.

IBC and Pennebaker's crew wanted nothing to do with the cubby hole. They wanted nothing less than to set up directly at the foot of the stage, to be part of it man. To feel the music, to see Dylan, to anticipate. 'AS' explained in his letter to Tito Burns -

'What causes me more concern, however, is the damage to the reputation of the Free Trade Hall. The patrons attending paid to hear and see a concert, not a recording session. If recording is to take place, the event should be so advertised, and the public not misled into paying good money for a concert, only to be annoyed by all the extraneous ritual of recording.'

'AS' displays a fine Northern sensibility by his concern over 'paying good money'. He then moves on to the nub of the matter -

'I was extremely annoyed myself by the arrogant and overbearing manner adopted by the persons employed on the recording. We were practically held to ransom - if recording was not permitted, then no concert - practically sums up the situation.

This just will not do ...'

It was clearly a case of 'when two cultures clash'. If 'AS' had succeeded in preventing recording taking place that night, this whole book would never have been. It's the distinct uniqueness of the unofficial recording that has created and preserved Manchester's place in Dylan's history - long live arrogant and overbearing manners!

The other major altercation that took place that afternoon inside the Free Trade Hall concerned the removal of the platform seats. Back to 'AS's' letter again -

'In the event, the equipment that was brought was so much that seats (already sold) had to be taken out and the patrons found alternative places. Also patrons on the platform seats were put to some disadvantage by reason of the equipment.'

'AS' felt it was all too much as he gazed at the jumble of cables and amplifiers. It was his civic duty to call in the Chief Fire Officer of Manchester to examine the mess and declare if the concert could go ahead. Perhaps this was 'AS's' only way of fighting back, his only way of preserving whatever fragile shards of authority that he still possessed. The only way he could maintain some dignity in the crawling sea of arrogance and Chaos that threatened to overwhelm him and his staff?

In full dress uniform the Chief Fire Officer duly led his team round the stage, probing, lifting, and asking awkward questions. No doubt Fred Perry would have done all the talking, smoothing things over, smiling in his cheerful way. The same way he always did when he was trying to get Dylan onstage on time. Fred's was a thankless job, but he got the job done and that was good enough for Grossman, Dylan, CBS and the Chief Fire Officer of Manchester. After questioning the unusual suspects and checking every wire it was decided - the concert could go ahead.

The Cause Of All The Trouble Arrives.

Dylan, Grossman and the rest of the crew arrived from The Midland Hotel at about 4 pm. The soundcheck got going straight away. They played 'Ballad of a Thin Man,' and 'Just Like Tom Thumb's Blues,' plus fragments of several others. With 'Thin Man,' was Dylan gearing up for a riposte to the inevitable onslaught of criticism that he knew was heading his way? Realistically, the answer has to be - no. It was simply the one number from the electric set where Dylan wasn't sited in front of the centre mike playing a guitar, harmonica and singing. On 'Thin Man' he moved to the side of the set up, stage right if you want to get technical, and played the grand piano that was until then being occupied by Richard Manuel. Rumour has it, but it can't be confirmed even to this very day, that Granada TV filmed the soundcheck. There's certainly a recording of 'Just Like Tom Thumb's Blues' taken from the afternoon session that's surfaced on several bootlegs, usually as a bonus track. Judging from its quality, the recording is in stereo, it would be a fair guess to say that it was one of the IBC tapes. A dry run presumably, before the night's taping?

With everything ready for the concert, Dylan, Grossman and the rest of the entourage went out of the back of the Free Trade Hall and got into two black Austin Princesses for the (very) short journey to the Midland Hotel, where black silk sheets had been laid on Dylan's bed, as per orders from Mr Grossman's management office.

As The Night Approaches

Rick Saunders arrived at the Free Trade Hall at around 6 pm. He was a student at Manchester University and, along with fellow students, John Runeckles and Mike Shade, had been hired to work as ushers for the night. Students, then as now, were perpetually short of money and all sorts of surprising jobs came along. Some hired themselves out for medical experiments, others, including Rick and myself, took on the filthy and dangerous task of unloading freight containers filled with bananas. It was filthy because you had to hoist the great stalks of fruit onto your shoulders and carry them to waiting lorries. It was dangerous because the tarantulas that had been blissfully asleep in the refrigerated holds of the merchant ships were now rudely awakened by you slinging them around and offering your shoulder as an unlikely perch. The containers were always full of nasty surprises. You can imagine how eagerly we awaited publication of Dylan's rumoured novel (*Tarantula*).

To supplement his grant Rick and his friends had managed to get themselves taken on as hired hands at the Free Trade Hall.

'We used to go to Barry Ansell's record shop (Barry's Record Rendezvous) on the bridge over to Salford. We used to go there to check out all the latest releases... Blues and stuff... Anything which was underground and hard to find. And he told us that they wanted workers at the Free Trade Hall. They'd asked him to get some students. Before Dylan we'd done it on two or three occasions. We were like ushers, taking tickets, guiding people to their seats, that kind of thing. One of them I remember was a slide show of Scotland! We didn't mind what it was because it was ten bob (50 pence) which was a lot of money in those days. But then when we heard Dylan was coming! There was a really big buzz going around.'

Rick was in the vanguard of people in the 1960s who liked music for its own sake, untroubled by factionalism or questions of 'authenticity'.

'The guy who introduced me to Dylan was one of the leading Marxists at the University, and they very much held Dylan to be one of their own. - a guy called Mike - and in my first year at University, at the end of 1963, I went round to his place and he played me Bob Dylan. I'd heard Peter, Paul and Mary, so I knew the name, I knew who he was. He was presented to us as a very heavy Leftist thing - in the tradition of Topic Records, Big Bill Broonzy, and The Weavers,. And I listened to him for a bit and it tied in with my more Libertarian ideals. I remember when *Another Side Of Bob Dylan* came out, the Marxists were beginning to drift away saying it was all a bit too personal. By 1966 there were a whole lot of questions being asked about Dylan - sort of "are you on the bus or off it?"'

There Are Those Who Disagree.

'Lonnie' doesn't want to give his second name. It's not that he's embarrassed about what he did that night, 32 years ago. He still feels he was right.

'My point's proved by Dylan playing for the Pope. That's all he's ever been into - money.'

It's just that Lonnie doesn't want the hassle. He agreed to talk to me in a pub in Salford where he has a job as a social worker.

'I first heard Dylan in 1963. I was living in Southport and I had this friend, Gary. His father was a Native American, full-blooded. The family had moved over to England because his dad was made European executive for the Rikoh Camera Company. They lived close by. It was quite funny really, here was his dad, wearing suits and flying round Europe all week and at the weekend he used to sit in a sweat lodge and take peyote!

'Anyway, Gary had this Bob Dylan record and I thought it was amazing. I couldn't believe this was a 21 year old, he sounded like a grizzled, old, black bluesman. When I moved to Manchester in 1964 I'd go to Folk clubs and there were other people there who liked Dylan as well. He spoke to us. Every song seemed relevant to what was happening in the world, what was happening to me. I was getting more involved with things like CND, though I stopped short of joining the Communist Party or anything like that. I was more of your traditional socialist, very working class. Always voted Labour, always will.'

Lonnie had gone to see Dylan in 1965.

'A whole bunch of us from the MSG (Manchester Sports Guild, a popular city centre Folk venue) went. It was alright, but you could see things were changing. He had that bloody awful single out ("Subterranean Homesick Blues"), and everywhere you looked was Pop music and stupid mindless drivel.'

If he felt that way about it, why did he go to the concert in 1966?

'We thought there might still be hope. A way of getting him to change his mind. That he hadn't completely sold out yet ... '

And There Again...

Dave Rothwell, who ran the Hollins College Folk club was also aware of the controversy surrounding Dylan.

'I was aware of it, but I didn't think he'd sold out. I enjoyed his music. I liked everything he did.'

As seven o'clock approached, Rick, Mike and John were sent to their positions at the concert hall's doors. Lonnie and the wrecking crew went for a drink in the Abercrombie pub near to the gig. Roger and Jane Harvey were looking for a place to park their car. The rest of us were beginning to mill around the entrance to the Free Trade Hall on Peter Street.

Stewart Tray had to wait at work until 6pm and could barely control his excitement -

'I'd left school at 15 and started work at Burtons (a gentlemen's outfitters). I couldn't concentrate at work at all that day, you know, just waiting for the concert. In those days you worked until six o'clock on the dot. It was terrible, wicked, wicked employers. Made my way to the Free Trade Hall and they wouldn't let anybody in. Jobsworths at the door and they were really looking at us, scowling at us, "What are you lot doing here, wanting to be let into the hall?" We pressed our faces up to the glass, watching and waiting. I knew our seats were unreserved so I thought the nearer we got to the door the better our chances of getting decent seats.... The guy eventually opened the door ...'

It seems strange now how people would wait in line in an orderly fashion for one single door to be opened, a door which several thousand people were waiting to pass, but just check out *Don't Look Back* for similar scenes at venues around Great Britain.

'... They looked at our tickets and took the whole thing. Didn't tear them or anything. We went in at those two doors near the foyer. I'd already been there the year before, I knew what to do. Straight up the side-steps and we plonked ourselves right down behind where Dylan would be. Right behind him. Then we waited for the concert to begin ... '

Paul Kelly:

'Me and a mate went into town together on the bus. We met up with everyone on the steps of the Free Trade Hall, and just seeing this huge crowd of people waiting to get in to see Bob Dylan was an amazing rush.'

Kevin Fletcher noticed how different the crowd was from the year before:

'We'd been to the pub at the back of the Free Trade Hall, and we went straight from there to the concert. There was a stall selling albums in the foyer, (clearly visible in the foyer footage of *Eat The Document*) badges and that sort of thing... The year before had been a typical Folk club thing. 1966 was a bit more dopey, the beginning of hippy... It was the length of the hair, the clothes. It had more of a Rock atmosphere to it.'

Dave Rothwell met his girlfriend, Ellie, and his mate Rob Hulton in town before making their way to the Free Trade Hall.

'When we got there the atmosphere was amazing. We handed in our tickets and filed upstairs and there was a bit of a buzz. When we sat down it all went quiet, just like it would for a classical concert... We were up on the balcony on the left hand side. It's amazing really because the Free Trade Hall used to have a bit of an ambience. We only used to go there for special occasions.... '

Kevin Fletcher:

'We thought there might be trouble because we'd read about it in the press. Even in *The Daily Mirror* or *The News Chronicle*, there'd been an article about booing at other concerts. Reports from Bristol or Newcastle, somewhere where people didn't approve of the electric band .'

'Mike King and I met outside the Free Trade Hall, on the steps along with nearly two thousand other people. There were no such things as Freaks yet, but the first glimmerings of a new age were upon us. As we milled around the foyer we gravitated towards a record stall. *Blonde On Blonde* wasn't on sale yet, but what blew our minds was a cardboard cut out of Dylan wearing shades and holding an electric guitar, with the legend - 'Bob Dylan Brings It All Back Home'. At the time, I would have cheerfully cut off my right arm to own one, but as I recognised the sales girls from Hime and Addison, it was with a sinking heart that I realised that if I asked them anything about it they'd tell me they knew nothing (while smiling pleasantly).'

Upon Arrival

The Traditionalists that Rick Saunders was talking about were there in force. Girls with long hair, young men with longer chins. I must have counted at least sixteen Suze Rotolos, twenty Joan Baezs. There were very few long haired men gathered there, but there were more than the year before.

Getting into the Free Trade Hall that evening though, wasn't proving so easy for a couple of our concertgoers -

'We got to the concert on the night and as we handed the tickets over at the door we should have gone in, right at the front, the gentleman collecting the tickets said, "Ah, we've been waiting for you."

Tim Green, Kath and their cousin Sandra, were completely taken aback by the reception they got.

'And we stood back a bit, and he said, "Would you just stand here a minute please?"'

By now they were beginning to get really paranoid. They'd bought their tickets in good faith from a reputable outlet but they were now feeling like criminals.

'And we said, "Yeah," and he just carried on letting people through. Then he went for some kind of security chap or something.'

By now their paranoia level was rising to the roof. What had they done wrong? Why wouldn't they let them in?

Finally the security man came along and told them that there was a problem with their seats.

'I said, "I can guarantee that they're genuine, they're not forgeries." And he said, "Oh, no. It's nothing like that. What's happened is we were expecting an acoustic Folk singer, and he's come with so much equipment that we've had to put the speakers down off the stage into the seating area." And the speakers actually took up the area where we were supposed to be. He said, "We've got a bit of a dilemma.... You can either demand your seats and stop the concert...."'

The implications of this took a moment to sink in for Kath and Tim....

"'Or, you can take the seats that we offer you.'"

Displaying remarkable social conscience, Tim and Kath decided.

'... We'd heard rumours of the trouble at concerts as we got the music papers. It wasn't going to stop us from going to this once in a lifetime opportunity. As we were queuing outside there'd been loads of rumours going round. "Oh, he got booed off the stage at Liverpool." All unofficial rumours going around... Well we wouldn't have been very popular if we'd stopped the concert, so we asked to see the new seats and Kath and myself managed to stay together. Sandra had a separate seat elsewhere. We were about four rows back.'

Things were even more complicated for Malcolm Metcalfe who hadn't got a ticket at all.

'I remember being interviewed outside, which I found quite unusual. And I remember watching the guy with the camera and stuff like that. I was thinking, "What is that?" I'd never seen that kind of thing before. I remember going in and being told there were no tickets. I was pretty devastated. I thought, "Jesus! I don't believe this"... So what happened was, I grew up in Salford, where basically I'd been getting into cinemas and stuff for all my life for nothing, with various tricks and things, you know. So my immediate thought was, there must be some way into this building, you know, I'm not having this. People went in and disappeared and I kind of walked around with a couple of other guys.... We came to this kind of a door, we gave it a kick and it just gave in. I just remember this corridor. It was quite long and painted a kind of cream colour. As soon as we got in, I could hear music. I could hear something going on. We crept along... and we crept up to those doors that had kind of little windows in. A couple of window doors. And I looked through and I was quite stunned because Dylan was only about ten yards away!'

Malcolm and the others stayed there throughout the concert undisturbed by security. They saw the entire evening, and we will rejoin them later.

'Five Minutes Bob'

There was an almost unwritten tradition that Dylan concerts would start slightly later than advertised. Birmingham on the 12th was delayed by 45 minutes owing to 'technical difficulties'. On the night before Manchester, the Sheffield Gaumont concert was delayed, this time because of a bomb warning. The ticket for the Free Trade Hall stated a 7-30 starting time. Dylan and the others had arrived back at the hall around 7 o'clock and were ensconced in the large dressing room behind the stage, the one usually used by the members of the Halle Orchestra. DA Pennebaker was prowling around the foyer shooting footage of the fans queuing to get in. As 7-20 approached Grossman was checking the box office receipts before going back to the dressing room to make sure everything was OK.

In the hall the audience was being guided to their seats by Rick Saunders and his fellow workers. Mike and I sat towards the back on the right hand side. Paul Kelly and his cohort positioned themselves four rows from the front in row DD, just off centre. Tim and Kath Green were in the same row but on the opposite side. Dave and Anne Rothwell filed upstairs onto the balcony where they could see all of the stage, including Stewart Tray who had manoeuvred himself onto the platform seats. Barbara Murray and her best friend, Doreen, were near the central aisle towards the middle of the stalls, which was roughly near where Lonnie and his friends were sat.

The overall atmosphere was hushed and reverent, but there was a palpable expectancy in the air. If anything, it was almost like being at a trial, waiting for the jury to come back with a verdict.

Most people were sat down, one or two were standing, probably looking for old friends. The ushers came and went. As 7-30 arrived everyone's attention became focused on the stage.

By the drum riser, Stewart worried that it might be just like the Joan Baez concert he'd been to the year before. She was 45 minutes late on stage, but tonight he needn't have worried.

Paul Kelly describes his feelings:

'There was a real expectation. It was like a buzz, a quiver much more than anything else... A low animated quiver... My eyes were absolutely glued to the stage entrance. It had a mucky, rusty red curtain ... '

At approximately 7-35 the house lights went down. The audience went totally quiet.

'... Then a single spot on stage and he came out but there was a light on behind him and I remember the corona of hair caught in it. To this day it was incredibly moving.... This was the bloke... This was the man himself in front of you....'

For me, it was a sheer thrill. At first I couldn't believe it was actually him, but there he was, walking up to the microphone. I strained to see what he looked like. The first thing to strike me was his hair. Up until that point all I had seen generally were year-old publicity shots, but here he was in the flesh and the hair - it was magnificent, an explosion of tangled curls. Under the spotlight it looked bright auburn, almost red. It bobbed up and down as he moved. Dylan's suit was an Edwardian-style, yellowy-brown tweed, buttoned all the way up. His boots were Cuban, his shirt was black and I was blown away.

Before the audience had finished applauding his appearance on stage, Dylan started strumming the chords to 'She Belongs To Me.'

Tim and Kath Green:

'... It just sent shivers down your back, to see this man that you'd been listening to for ages... We were just in awe. To be honest we were looking forward to it so much he could have turned out a load of rubbish and in my head it still would have been perfect.... It was just the fact of being there ... He was a legend ... '

Rick Saunders felt the same thing from where he was standing:

'It didn't take me a minute to snap into it. I thought it was lovely. He just had an aura about him - you could just see it pouring out from every pore, so to speak. He did it perfectly and he filled the whole hall... I thought it was just lovely.'

Lonnie:

'The first half was pretty good. It was nice to hear the old songs. Very much like the previous year, but there wasn't the same bite to it, if you know what I mean?'

She Belongs To Me

For his fans, and maybe for Dylan himself, this song is a strong opener to the acoustic set. It should have been immediately familiar to anybody who was aware of Dylan's output. Written towards the end of 1964 and re-corded in January 1965 it had been part of Dylan's live repertoire since March 27th of that year when he performed it at the Civic Auditorium,

Santa Monica. It came out on *Bringing It All Back Home*, that same
month. Dylan was to use it as his opening acoustic number throughout the
nine months of the Tour.

'She Belongs To Me' is magical and mystical. Paul Williams has described it as an 'invocation' and he is correct. It corresponds to a traditional occult framework of invocation for worshipping the Goddess/Isis,
call Her what you will. Just as an exercise in analysis, let's examine this
song from a mystical perspective. There are interesting correspondences
in its construction that relate to some of the things we know were going on
in Dylan's life at the time.

According to Scaduto, Dylan met Sarah Lowndes in late 1964, which would tie in with the period the song was written in. Allen Ginsberg was responsible at the time for introducing Dylan to a broader, more eclectic set of mystical influences, the I Ching, Zen and Mahayana Buddhism, amongst other things. Sarah too was into mysticism. Dylan described her to Robert Shelton as 'holy'. Others said she was a very together woman, 'ego-less in a Zen kind of way'. Maybe then, to Dylan, she did have everything she needed?

This, then, is no ordinary love song. Its impact on Popular song has possibly never been fully estimated. Nowhere does the word 'love' figure in the lyrics. What we do get is a vision of a man under the spell of an enchantress, though its lyrical sophistication is light years ahead of any of the contemporary tunes that smeared their way round the Pop charts at the time, or even for a long time afterwards. Its sister song on *Bringing It All Back Home*, 'Love Minus Zero/No Limit' is of equal measure. They were both responsible for a redefining of the parameters of Popular Music

Technically the format follows the simplicity of a standard 12-bar with the first line repeated then verse closure ensured by the introduction of the last line. It is a format possessed of an elegant texture that belies the apparent simplicity. It has a richness and complexity of construction that opens itself out on many levels, which is what mystical song-writing should be all about.

First, the Goddess is called by use of a description of Her attributes, physical and mental. This woman artist has a magic so strong that She can bring light to the darkness and turn daylight black. She has the power to fundamentally reverse the natural order of things. She is incapable of falling as She flies so high above the narrator of the song. The fact that She's nobody's child again suggests a psychic dimension to Her being.

The final verse is an instruction of how to worship Her. The Goddess must be given offerings on two specific holy days, Halloween and the Winter Solstice. The presents are both intrinsic to magical ceremonies, trumpets and drums being used for drawing down and dismissing respectively.

In his performance of this song at the Free Trade Hall, Dylan weaves the lyrics in and out with a fluidity that's only excelled by his harmonica breaks. The final one in particular, the one that brings the tune to its conclusion, has long, drawn out notes that entice the listener further in rather than deflecting them away. Although he's performed the song dozens of times before over the last nine months and more, Dylan still manages to bring a freshness and vitality to it and the audience applause at the end of the song is warm and appreciative.

Fourth Time Around

The soundtrack to a movie that never got made. Dylan's second song of the set is the one that made John Lennon paranoid. Lennon thought Dylan was parodying his efforts at diversification in 'Norwegian Wood,' though he later described it as 'great'. The main melody certainly is a lift from 'Norwegian Wood,' but Dylan takes it further by bringing in a minor key change. If the song was an homage, he certainly transcends the world of St John's Wood media groupie-dom that Lennon was singing about. An interesting side point is that Lennon stated he wrote 'Norwegian Wood' during what he called his 'Dylan phase', in which case when Dylan played McCartney the acetate of 'Fourth Time Around,' the wheel had gone in an ironic full circle. Whatever, here we get a narrative that is so full of ideas and images that it could drive you to distraction thinking of who you'd like to put in the roles of male/female lovers.

There's been a row and the woman screams that all his words are just lies. The argument degenerates into a fight with insults being hurled around all over the room ('a screaming battleground'?), and the singer taps on her drum. As she straightens herself up he feels in his pocket for his very last piece of gum, which in a gesture of reconciliation he offers to her. She throws him out but he's forgotten his shirt and has to go back and knock. The outraged woman makes him wait in the hallway while she goes to get it and he idly stands around trying to make sense of a surreal photograph she has of herself in a wheelchair.

When she comes back he tries to make up to her again, but can't resist insulting her by telling her that he can't understand her words because of the gum she's chewing. This time she screams at him so much she goes into a swoon and the singer takes the opportunity to check out her things before he leaves.

At the end of the song he goes back to his first love, armed with trophies, but ends up warning her not to ask for anything off him because he doesn't want anything off her.

This is an unusual song for the period (written and recorded in 1966), inasmuch as there is very little of the lyrical playfulness, or surrealism, that we could expect from Dylan. The characters are fairly straightforward, there are no tea-preachers or phantoms, or little girls lost. It appears that they are simply two lovers who have fallen out after a blazing argument. If it was a dig at The Beatles, it works because it demonstrates one thing that Dylan can do superbly, and that is to turn an ordinary event into something quite magnificent by his mastery of language. The apparent simplicity is underlayed by an astonishing sophistication of technique.

'Fourth Time Around' certainly created confusion at the Free Trade Hall. It hadn't been released in England yet, *Blonde On Blonde* was still a short time away (financially, if not physically), and in the space provided in the programme for you to fill in the order of the songs, it appears to have been notated by at least several people as 'Jamaican Rum'. This is entirely understandable as it was practically the only frame of reference in the song that an English audience could latch onto. All the way through Dylan's performance of 'Fourth Time Around' we were straining to catch hold of lyrics. There weren't any cassette recorders around in those days. Any audience bootlegs from the period were usually done on Woolworth's reel to reels that consumed batteries like there was no tomorrow. Very few of us had them anyway. What Mike King and I did for days after the concert was to try and write down snatches, fragments of those lyrics we could remember. It was another world then.

When Dylan started playing he shifted quickly from the 'C'/'F' riff into a minor key. Then he started playing the harmonica before he started to sing. On the recording his voice is husky and slightly breathless. Straight notes are turned into grace notes. He bends and shapes them at his own command. The song is delivered impassionately despite the ferocity of the events described. All of it, as I have said, was entirely new to us. It is a song that demands attention. You have to listen to the lyrics (as, of course, one has to do with any song by Dylan), but here was a new number that therefore was possessed by an urgency all of its own. At the end of the narrative Dylan shifted back to harmonica again. Single notes that replicated the chord structure runs, extemporising over the melody line. And then, almost as soon as it had begun, 'Fourth Time Around' had finished.

One of the main problems associated with being a performing artist is that people inevitably want to hear the songs that they are familiar with. Here we have a situation with Dylan of an artist whose creative output far outstripped the time he had available on stage. 'Fourth Time Around' had only been recorded in February of that year, yet Dylan was already using it as his second number by March 1966. Realistically he could have performed an entire set of numbers from *Blonde On Blonde* if he had so desired. But audiences dictate which way a set will go and many an artist has fallen foul of the crowd by trying to present numbers that they've never heard before. It's to Dylan's credit that he tried to mix and match a varied selection from his output throughout this period.

Visions Of Johanna

The third number would also outwit the assembled crowd. 'Visions Of Johanna' wouldn't surface on an English release until a month later. I remember hearing it, the recorded version, late at night on a radio programme called 'The Simon Dee Show', some weeks after the concert. Up to that point, which confirmed that it was out on record, I'd never been sure I would ever hear it again, and that would have been unimaginably frightening. There are certain moments in history when it's been an astonishing joy to be alive and on the planet, specific instances when you've been allowed to share true genius with an artist. On two occasions Dylan has had that effect on me.

The first occasion was hearing 'Like A Rolling Stone' for the first time. Jesus, what a blast that was! Imagine being fifteen, switching on the radio and hearing - that tune! The second was hearing 'Visions Of Johanna'. Nothing in our lives had prepared us for the sheer brilliance of this number. OK, we'd had 'Tambourine Man' and 'Gates Of Eden,' et al, but this number took us far beyond anything we'd ever experienced before. This was LSD, before it became a product to be marketed and pushed out as an item available for mass consumption, via the proselytising laid on by Timothy Leary and Allen Ginsberg. Sensing this perhaps, ten days later,

Dylan made a statement about it before he performed the song at the Albert Hall.

'I'm not going to play anymore concerts here in England, and I'd just like to say that it's all wrong.... This is probably one song (bear in mind that it hadn't been released in England yet) that your English music press here would call "a drug song". Well I don't... I don't write "drug songs". I never have. I wouldn't know how to go about it... I'm not saying this for any kind of defence, or reason, or anything like that....'

Melody Maker carried on reporting Dylan's Albert Hall speech with the following:

'I like all my old songs. It's just that things change all the time. Everybody knows that. I never said they were "rubbish" (for some reason Dylan delivered this in a 'Northern' accent.) That's not in my vocabulary....

'This music you are going to hear - if anyone has any suggestions on how it could be played better, or how the words could be improved... ? We've been playing this music since we were ten years old. Folk music was just an interruption and was very useful. If you don't like it, that's fine.

'This is not English music you are listening to. You haven't really heard American music before. I want now to say that what you are hearing is just songs. You're not hearing anything else but words and sounds. You can take it or leave it. If there is something that you disagree with, that's great.'

'I'm sick of people asking: "What does it mean?" It means nothing.'

If this is what Dylan said, and these are the words as reported by Britain's leading Rock paper of the time, then, in a bizarre way, why couldn't he have said them so clearly and precisely before. Say around the time he played Newport? It would have cleared up an awful lot of misunderstanding and in the long run, saved an awful lot of heartache. However, he didn't. And maybe I'm quite wrong to read 'Visions Of Johanna' as an hallucination-atory song.

Here, ten days after the Free Trade Hall, we have Dylan emphatically denying the use of any form of hallucinogenics or stimulants or opiates in the construction of any of his numbers, and who are we to argue? What is clear, however, is that 'Visions Of Johanna' was a song that transcended anything in the Pop oeuvre at the time.

On November 30th 1965, he and the Band made their first attempts to cut the number variously known as 'Seems Like A Freeze Out,' 'Freeze Out' and, eventually, 'Visions Of Johanna.' It's generally agreed that the first version of the song was an up-tempo Rock style attack, which later surfaced on a number of bootlegs. This is a first try at a number that was to eventually become a definitive Dylan song and, as such, bears repeated listening as an indicator of his process of song-writing and recording.

After seven attempts Dylan decided to hang loose. He wasn't getting the sound that he heard inside his head and it wasn't until January that further sessions finally uncovered the meaning that Dylan had buried within the number. And yet, already he was apparently so excited by the structure of the song that he decided to include it as an acoustic number, premiering it on December 3rd 1965, at Berkeley. Sadly, no record of that acoustic set has survived.

New York was the site for more sessions after the six-week Christmas break (surely long needed?), but again, even though this later version of 'Freeze Out' was slowed down, the alchemy of Dylan's vision failed to materialize. It wasn't until Dylan flew to Nashville on January 26th 1966 and Bob Johnson wheeled in the Nashville session players that contributed so much towards the crystallisation of Dylan's musical ideas at the time that a definitive version was cut. This is the one that we can hear now on *Blonde On Blonde*.

Visions still staggers me now after all these years. At first it seemed like a song driven by the Deep South. Many of the lines shimmered with a kind of heat haze that can only be brought on by total proximity to the sub-tropical temperatures of Florida, or Georgia. Then, it developed, as if by an organic process, another view of the geography of America. A psycho-geographical view, where sense and time were suspended, a mental process that demanded a re-appraisal acquainted with a re-mapping of America along emotional lines. Perhaps the recording of the song in studios as far apart as Nashville and New York contributed to this.

Dylan is stranded, maybe in a New York loft. He acts as a voyeur while a couple make love, but he, the singer, is definitely on his own. But even as he watches Louise and her lover his thoughts turn to Johanna. Maybe Louise is a hooker? Maybe Louise is just another all-night girl trying to outwit the night watchman? Then Dylan produces one of the most memorable and enigmatic images in the history of rock lyrics - 'The ghost of electricity howls from the bones in her face!'

These words had a resonance that went beyond the melody to which they were sung. The meaning of the phrase is not clear, and yet the words vibrate, swinging their sweet song from the subconscious. Words are the shrouds that we wrap breath in, and even as they die on our tongues, these words take on a life of their own. So with this line, its jarring other worldly image leaps out from beyond the song's confines to jolt and shock.

By the third verse Dylan broadens his observations to include another, mysterious male figure, 'Little Boy Lost'. He's the kind of guy who wallows in self pity and brags of his misery. In the ensuing lines, Dylan berates him for his selfishness and hopelessness. He then finishes the verse by screaming (literally in the alternate takes), how hard it is to go on, and how the hallucinations have kept him, up past daylight.

For the fourth verse, maybe we're all stuck in New York? We're forced into museums where the exhibits last forever (Infinity?). Then, Dylan becomes specific - making a statement about Leonardo Da Vinci's Mona Lisa and the enigmatic nature of her smile. He then pulls the image back into our vision by relating the icon to Marcel Duchamp's scurrilous reproduction of Leonardo's picture - LHOOQ (it's French slang for 'She's got a really hot ass') - Mona Lisa with a moustache, 'Hear the one with the moustache say "Jeeze, I can't find my knees!"'

Of course not. She's a painting! And not only is she artifice, a facsimile, a reproduction, she is there to be drawn, re-designed and painted over. The jewels and binoculars that adorn the head of the mule in this song are prime examples of Dylan's symbolic imagery. Later, they were perfectly reproduced as a photograph by the Rolling Stones for the cover of their live album *Get Yer Ya's Out*.

The final verse sees us and Dylan back in the world of Louise, who should not be the focus of a song ostensibly about Johanna. Yet, when we look closer, Louise becomes the centrifuge of Dylan's imagery, the locus of our fantasy. In this final verse the rich images build to a crescendo in a supernova of astrological vibrancy. The Madonna is Virgo. The exploding fish truck extols Pisces. The fiddler himself is Mercury, who becomes Thoth, who becomes The Fool. All is Chaos and, as Dylan said, 'I embrace chaos. I'm not sure whether it embraces me.'

Enigma then reigns supreme in the apocalyptic imagery of 'Johanna.' All that the minstrel has left at the end of the song are images, and that is all that we as an audience in 1966 were left with.

Perhaps what is most significant, considering the lengths to which Dylan was going to reproduce on stage the wild new sounds he was hearing in his head, is that Dylan felt that this song was so important to his new canon that we were to be treated to it without the benefit of electrical accompaniment. Here was a song that stated his intent without recourse to embellishment of any kind. It was, purely and simply, a song about a situation, a feeling, an idea. And that the power of the song was so great that it had to be sung no matter what. Dylan did sing it throughout the tour. The reactions that it got were generally favourable, occasionally rhapsodic.

And so, there we were in 1966, listening to Dylan performing a number called 'Visions Of Johanna,' that none of us had ever heard before and, quite likely, never expected to hear again.

It's All Over Now, Baby Blue

Once again the audience are on friendly territory. Dylan had performed 'Baby Blue' as his final number in his concert a year before at the Free Trade Hall, and the reception then had been more than welcoming. The album it had been featured on, *Bringing It All Back Home* had been available for just over a year, and was a best seller in the English album charts.

The song itself was another signpost in the redirection of Dylan's career, leaving behind the stepping stones of 'protest' and carrying forward the observational ideas that appear to lie behind many of the songs on the album. It was a whole new world, but by now, to his listeners, a familiar one by dint of age.

This is another of Dylan's most enigmatic songs. The lyrics weave a series of patterns that the listeners make of what they will. This was a brave move at that point in Rock's history. Where pop songs would be unambiguous and clear cut: I love you, you love me, precise indicators, seldom possessed of any depth or mystery; Dylan by contrast, had no message to import, and did not challenge the listener to find meaning in the songs, or search for hidden mystical messages. He simply wanted people to listen to them and enjoy them without fear. Just let the images make their own impression.

In 'Baby Blue' Dylan takes us on a journey across a flat landscape of the soul - populated by orphans and artists, seasick sailors. Reindeer armies trudge relentlessly across the vista while the dead stay where they are. As an ex-lover walks away, a vagabond takes her place and raps on the door wearing Baby Blue's clothes. Then comes the pay-off line - it may all be over, but you have to start anew.

One of the frequently asked questions regarding this song is, who is Baby Blue? Both Robert Shelton and Paul Williams are of the view that Dylan is looking at himself in this song. Others have suggested it was a reference to David Blue, a Village contemporary, now known by his original name David Cohen. Of course, it might just be about nobody, but I would have to broadly agree with Shelton and Williams. It is a song about change and moving on and as such fits perfectly to the situation in which Dylan was in at the time. Dylan, himself, mischievously refers to an old Gene Vincent song as the source of inspiration.

In Manchester that night, Dylan turns in a good, if not revelatory, performance of the song. He doesn't sound bored with it; nor does he sound excited by it. There's a momentary gap before he starts playing while he tunes down his bottom E string and then he launches off into the number. Using the bass as a drone in this way gives the song an old time feel. The repeated fingering of grace notes on the higher strings lend it an air that sounds reminiscent of an Appalachian dulcimer.

Dylan's voice is precise. His articulation of the lyrics is carefully stressed. Every syllable, every line and every nuance fits perfectly into the droning dulcimer-like scheme. Dylan's harmonic playing too is at its best, both in the break after the third verse and in the final harmonica solo with which the song ends. Once again Dylan's virtuosity on this instrument is clearly demonstrated. The break has a structure reminiscent of old lace. It is gossamer thin, interwoven like an ornate spiders web. It stretches and spirals into the infinite landscape of the song.

Desolation Row

'Desolation Row' is the apocalyptic carnival at the world's end. This is where we'll all end up one day. It is neither Heaven nor Hell, suggesting more a place of purgatory where the tortured and the damned stagger through their penitances, condemned forever to repeat their aimless wanderings and pointless rituals. The characters who inhabit 'Desolation Row' read like a cast-list for a nightmare filmed by Luis Bunuel on a set designed by Salvador Dali. The blind commissioner, Cinderella, Einstein disguised as Robin Hood, Ophelia, Doctor Filth, Casanova, Ezra Pound and TS Eliot, all of them wander haplessly past Dylan's withering gaze.

This song is relentlessly dark. It is an epic poem on a par with Allen Ginsberg's *Howl* as a vision of modern American dystopianism. It reeks of Hollywood and comic books, Saturday morning TV and English Literature classes. It also reeks of the Bible and the Torah, of opium and starlight, but above all, it reeks of helplessness.

If *Bringing It All Back Home* had offered a kind of sop to the die-hard Traditionalists by keeping one side within the realms of acoustic presentation, its follow up, *Highway 61 Revisited*, held out no hope at all. It was pretty well pure electricity, with the exception of the final cut on the album, 'Desolation Row,' which has bass and acoustic lead guitar backing for Dylan's guitar and harmonica. Clinton Heylin offers either Mike Bloomfield or Bruce Langhorne as lead guitar.

There is, however, another version, recorded earlier, this time with electric guitar played by Nashville session man Charlie McCoy, who Dylan had flown into New York especially for the occasion.

The McCoy version is a much more sombre and funereal take than the one to get released on the album. Both versions have much to recommend them - what remains a mystery is why Dylan felt it necessary to go back into the studio and redo the song.

Presumably the majority of the audience in Manchester that night would have been familiar with the tune. Although Dylan hadn't played it live in the UK until the 1966 tour, he had been featuring it as part of the acoustic

set in America since August 28th of the previous year, and it had been available in Britain on record since around that time. At over eleven minutes in length it was a tour de force in Dylan's live act. At times it felt like watching a tightrope walker, balancing, then skipping, then balancing again as the monologue relentlessly rolled on. It was simply quite staggering to be present and listen to the composer sing this. It felt at times more like being present at a Classical concert than a gig by a 'popular artiste'. Or maybe, more like being at a poetry reading, or a church service, so quiet and respectful were the audience (up to that point anyway!). People sat for concerts in those days and you gave your complete, undivided attention to the performer.

Dylan's performance of 'Desolation Row' at the Free Trade Hall is something quite beautiful, no wonder it held our attention for so long. Dylan used an almost lilting vocal quality that completely altered the timbre of his delivery. It was mesmerising and valedictory simultaneously. He played around with the rhythmic structure of the melody in apparently contradictory ways, a portent for the future direction his muse would carry him in. The artist who endlessly rebuilds himself.

After nearly nine minutes of singing Dylan allows the harmonica in. This time, however, he vamps whole chords, rather than using single notes. Up and down, up and down, relentlessly bringing in the changes. He brings the sung part of the tune to an end with the final verse and then reprises his harmonica solo. This time he uses bent single notes to stretch the framework laid down by the guitar chords, and then, eleven minutes and fifty three seconds after starting 'Desolation Row,' he brings it to its conclusion leaving an audience thrilled, hypnotised and knocked out.

Just Like A Woman

Dylan presumably wrote this song during the Christmas layoff and then went to Nashville to record it for *Blonde On Blonde*. It's listed as having been cut at Columbia's Music Row Studio on March 8th 1966, and it made its live debut at the Pacific National Exhibition Agrodome in Vancouver BC, on March 26th. And there it stayed in the acoustic set for the rest of the tour. In effect then, nobody had heard this song prior to seeing Dylan perform it. Again, I can remember being amazed by it. Outraged at its seeming simplicity and yet baffled by its obvious complexity. 'Just Like A Woman' lingered in my mind for a thousand years before I could buy it on disc a couple of months later. It was the hook, the chorus, the repetition and the cutting edge grace that carved through me.

Dylanologists have argued long and hard over the question - who is she? Who was Dylan singing about? The perceived wisdom is that the Girl/Woman of the song's lyric was Edie Sedgwick, who, it has been argued quite forcibly, was also Dylan's muse for 'Like A Rolling Stone.' Edie was a 'poor little rich girl' who had found a career of sorts in Andy

Warhol's Factory movies. In mid 1965 she told Warhol that she was going to be managed by Albert Grossman and she had taken to bringing Dylan round to the Factory. He'd even done a screen test for Warhol. It lies somewhere now, tied up in an executor's vault.

Some sources believe that Dylan and Edie were an item even when he was courting, marrying and impregnating Sarah Lowndes. They were certainly out and about in New York night clubs as late as December 28th 1965. It would seem that Dylan finished the affair around New Year and the song was possibly written shortly afterwards. Edie was apparently half furious and half-flattered when she heard it.

Dylan starts off with one of the greatest opening lines of any song - 'Nobody feels any pain'. Is this one of the greatest ironic statements in the history of the universe? Everybody feels pain of some sort at some time or another. To deny this in the opening of a song is to almost deny the very existence of reality. The line's very absurdity would make any other song writer reject it out of hand, and yet here's Dylan stating it as if it was an absolute, immutable truth of the cosmos. Dylan throws us out of kilter with the next line where we find him standing in the rain, we guess, outside from her place wondering how he got there. He then talks to us as confidantes, allowing us into the spoiled relationship to see it, as it were from his perspective. He says that everybody sees certain things of her that point to affluence and success, but he has begun to view her from a new angle and he is no longer sure that he likes what he sees. Her ribbons and her bows have fallen as if from in front of his eyes.

The tune is permeated by wonderful Country picking by Dylan. The vocal is rough and a little hoarse but it all adds up to present the argument of a wet, defeated lover, standing outside the social circle that his lover inhabits. Precisely picked, sung and accompanied by the ever present harmonica, the song drenches us with pathos and sadness. He sings clearly of her 'fog, amphetamine and pearls', and we have a pocket portrait of a young woman on the edge of a cataclysmic fall. Tiny, fragmented harmonica breaks punctuate the verses and lead up to the middle eight. There is a heartfelt poignancy when Dylan delivers the line 'Ain't it clear that I just don't fit?' It is a desperate plea for release from a relationship that has crumbled and collapsed. Why live in a sea of hurt?

The final harmonica solo is extended, delicate and passionate. Dylan's ability to wring such emotion from such a seemingly simple instrument is inspiring.

Mr Tambourine Man

This had been one of Dylan's concert stalwarts since May 1964 when he premiered it at the Royal Festival Hall on the 17th. He'd started writing it on his return from the New Orleans Mardi Gras, which may have also given him some of the inspiration for 'Chimes Of Freedom.' Again, it's a song that alerts us to the emancipation of Dylan's mind and style of writing. This is when he began to write songs about his own personal experiences rather than acting as some kind of reporter on current events. It is a liberation. On the *Highway 61 CD Rom* we are given a chance to hear it performed as a duet with Jack Elliot, taken from a session that was closer to the recording of *Another Side of Bob Dylan* than *Bringing It All Back Home,* where it eventually made its appearance as a solo number. There is also an earlier prototype on an unreleased Whitmark demo where Dylan accompanies himself on piano.

There is another suggestion that Dylan began work on 'Mr Tambourine Man' at Joan Baez's rented house at Big Sur, in California. There certainly seem to be allusions to the kind of freedom of mind and space that a place like Big Sur can induce in people. Whatever, the importance of this tune lies in the immediate success and impact that it made on Dylan's listeners. It has become a classic of the 20th century, cited and quoted by sources as varied as Presidents of nations and school teachers. And while he had already established himself as a major artist in his own right, Dylan's popularity was immeasurably increased by the success of The Byrds' version of 'Mr Tambourine Man' which was a top ten hit around the world. With this song Dylan had arrived.

With this song Dylan managed to completely capture the zeitgeist of the time. He locked into the spiritual feeling of an entity that was crawling out of the hidebound chaos of post-war reality and building a beachhead into the future. For a generation that had gone beyond the lies and hypocrisy of the antediluvian past, it was an era when there were limitless paths to choose from. Dylan signposted one way. There were movers, shakers and the Tambourine Man. We went a following.

It had truly become the closest thing to a Dylan anthem that he had yet created, outstripping even 'The Times They Are A Changing.' It had served as the final number for the first half of his set since Forest Hills the previous August, and now too at Manchester.

It took him a little time to get the number rolling on May 17th. He strums, he coughs, he plays his harmonica, he strums some more and then, finally, he is ready to begin. The words tumbled out as fresh as if he'd just written them - 'Hey, Mr Tambourine man play a song for me'. Where was the evening's empire that had vanished from Dylan's hand? Where were the ancient, empty streets that he sang so eloquently about? We too longed to take a trip. We too waited for our boot heels to go wandering.

Dylan's delivery in Manchester is short, precise, even sharp, the words nearly spat out. Not because he was bored with them but because that is what circumstance dictated. They needed a machine gun style of delivery in order for the full effectiveness of their meaning to be punched home where they belonged - in our heads. His harmonica playing once again exceeded all previous solos. The level of virtuosity was astonishing. Dylan's tonal control is something that almost defies belief.

Listening to the recording of that night creates within me almost the same level of transcendence that Dylan appears to have reached in the creation of the song. It is too formidable to challenge. Dylan, the Tambourine Man, takes us for that trip, out there on the beach beneath the diamond sky to a place that I could never have dreamt of.

Intermission

CHAPTER SEVEN
How Does It Feel?

As inconspicuously as he had come on stage, Dylan departed for the intermission. When the applause died down the house lights came up on an audience tense with mixed emotions. Lonnie and his crowd was on a high, brought on, so they saw it, by Dylan's apparent capitulation to sense.

'We thought, 'Great! He's done it'. You could see all this equipment on stage and he hadn't used it! We went off to the bar and we were all chatting away about how good he'd been and how glad we were that he'd done it solo. We just didn't think he'd dare come back on with a group.'

Kath and Tim stayed in the hall -

'We didn't leave the room. We stayed where we were. We didn't dare go out, we just sat and waited. We didn't even say very much. It was the be all and end all of anything that that we'd ever wanted to do... We were still taking it in when he'd gone off. We'd actually seen the person we idolised... Just the fact that we were there. He was a legend.'

All through the first half Paul Kelly had been taking photographs -

'When he started playing I felt, I felt the intensity. This is it. This is wonderful. I was taking photographs, so as well as listening I was trying to focus the camera. In my confusion I set the speed wrong for the first half dozen shots. I was listening, concentrating as I've never concentrated at a concert before or since. And there was Dylan 20 feet away. It was like having him in your living room. During the intermission the buzz was like a dam bursting. Everyone was holding their breath then loads of talking. There was a lot of talking about which song was which.'

I sat in my seat, paranoid about missing a moment, shaken by what I'd already seen and breathless with anticipation for what might come next. On the stage roadies scurried around as I desperately tried to remember lines from the new songs I'd just heard. People began drifting back to their seats and settling down. Albert Grossman called for Rick Saunders to come to the side of the stage.

'He looked like a degenerate Southern gentleman in his cream coloured suit, with his strange wispy long hair and enormous body. He was a very lurid character and he approached me and said, "You go up there." And I said, "What? What?" And he was pointing at the stage. And he said, "Protect Bob." - Looking back it was hyping up the occasion, very Malcolm McLaren. Even if you're not expecting any trouble, make out you are and it'll increase the juice.

'I'll tell you about Grossman though. Earlier that year I'd been to Stockholm and I went to an Odetta concert and I recognised the guitarist. I thought, that's the guy who played on "Mr Tambourine Man," and we found out it was Bruce Langhorne and we went and had a chat with him. I thought he was one of the best lead guitarists I'd heard, he sounded so good. I said to Grossman, "Why isn't Bruce Langhorne here?" thinking he should have been in the band, because I had no idea who they were. They were complete strangers. And Grossman said, "Oh, I believe we may have used him once or twice". And I thought, "you bastard"... And yet I thought Grossman was very impressive. There you were trying to be friendly and he just told you to "fuck off kid". It was impressive.'

Rick duly took his place on the side of the stage, facing the audience and waited for Dylan and the band's arrival.

A Quick Word About The Name

When news of the tour was first covered in the English music press it was stated that Dylan would be bringing a backing band with him. There was some speculation as to who would be in it and what their name would be. Very few people, if any, in Britain had heard of Ronnie Hawkins and The Hawks, nor their association with Dylan. Things in their homeland of

Canada were different however and, when playing with Dylan, the band were recognised and written about as Levon And The Hawks.

In Australia they were generally referred to simply as 'an electric backing group'. None of the posters for the tour in England or Australia mention any one else other than Dylan, but for the concert in Copenhagen the poster clearly states 'Bob Dylan with Levon And The Hawks.' There is a slight irony in the billing in that Levon Helm had actually quit the tour in 1965!

When Dylan arrived in England *Melody Maker* claimed he was being backed by 'the Group'. A week or so later they carried an article featuring an interview with Robbie Robertson in which he stated that they had no name at all.

Finally, just to confuse things even more in a news snippet in *Record Mirror*, Dylan was reported as saying the group were called The Crackers. In fact Helm, Robertson and friends didn't officially adopt the name 'The Band' until after they'd recorded their debut album in 1968, and even then, according to Helm, this was 'just so they can file it in the stores.'

The Second Half

Just before 8-50 pm the house lights dimmed and the stage spot came back on. So did a group of musicians. Mickey Jones climbed onto his drum riser and settled himself behind the kit. Robbie Robertson and Rick Danko plugged their guitars in and started tuning. Garth Hudson sat at the organ and Richard Manuel sat at the grand piano. People in the audience shifted nervously in their seats and looked around at one another trying to gauge reactions.

Dylan came back on stage with a black Fender guitar and plugged into an amp next to Robertson's. As they tuned up Hudson played a jaunty version of 'In An English Country Garden' on the upper register of the organ. After 12 seconds of tuning Dylan began the opening riff. We waited. The riff went on, finding a groove, settling in. Dylan and Robertson faced each other, hunched over their guitars looking like two gunslingers from a crazy movie that hadn't even been made yet. Then, amazement, as Dylan's body began to bounce up and down in time to the riff. Consternation amongst the Traditionalists. From his vantage point on the platform seats Stewart Tray got a good look at the band.

'I saw Hudson first, because he's quite a distinctive guy, you know. And Richard Manuel, and they all looked a bit mad. Tough. As if to say, "Let's see what reaction we get".'

These guys were clearly not folk musicians. They were all dressed in velvet suits. Danko's was maroon, the others were purple, green, beige and blue. It was all a bit strange. English Beat groups had just about stopped wearing matching stage outfits and here was the Rebel god with his demon crew kitted out like they were playing a resort in the Catskills. J

And then, presumably having found the groove Robertson did a quick count in. There was an almighty crash and they blasted off.

'They struck out into "Tell Me Momma" and it was loud for '66. Very loud. A huge noise, but very clear.'

'I couldn't believe it. It was so loud it physically hurt me.'

'It was loud!'

'... I felt like I was being forced back into my seat, you know? Like being in a jet when it takes off.'

'The level of sound was something that I'd never heard before, especially being so close up to it. I was just blasted out of my skin. It was physical rather than just listening to music. It took a long time before I could recognise what the tunes were.'

From his vantage point by the side stage door Malcolm Metcalfe kept watching.

'We kept peeping through the windows and every now and then we'd open the doors and get a blast of sound. We were frightened of opening the doors too often in case we got sussed... We stayed there throughout the concert. It was just great being there.'

Rick Saunders wondered if his job was as good as it had seemed when he was offered it.

'I was just alarmed at the thought that I was going to be pulled to pieces by an enraged mob as soon as it started... "Tell Me Momma," I'd never heard it before. None of us in the hall had ever heard it before - I was aware of a restlessness and a clashing in the air...'

More amazing still was Dylan. This was no longer the almost motionless troubador who had remained so stoically still throughout the first set. Here, now, in front of us an incarnation of the Dharma body of the Buddha that had hitherto been denied us. A Dylan the likes of which the most fervent of Traditionalists could only have come across in his/her wildest dreams. Dylan and his Fender, spitting in the eye of everybody who dared deny his vision, and grooving on it.

Lonnie:

'I couldn't believe it. It was all your worst nightmares coming true. He looked like Mick Jagger, posturing and strutting. It was all the worst elements of Pop. Like a parody only it wasn't - and it wasn't even funny.'

Other people were more open-minded. Steve Currie, for instance -

'I didn't know what to expect of Dylan and a band. I'd heard the music before on record and it sounded wonderful, but on the night - it was GREAT!!!'

Keith Fletcher:

'"Tell Me Momma" was excellent. I didn't know the song. It had a really good riff you could get hold of. I thought, this is interesting, I don't know this one. Yes, it was instantly likeable, I thought. And I thought from where I was sitting the sound was good. Maybe a bit rough, but that was fine, I didn't mind at all.'

Tell Me Momma

This song made its first appearance at White Plains in New York State on February 5 1966 on the opening leg of the world tour. As the first number of the electric set it's a bone-crushing aural assault. The tune hadn't been recorded, nor, as far as we know, has it ever been, so audiences were totally unfamiliar with it.

The number is the bastard child of Dylan's own 'From A Buick 6' and the swamp fever madness of Bo Diddley's 'Who Do You Love?' Maybe the song's directed at the same woman? The one who walks like Bo, but don't need no crutch? All three songs have cemeteries and bones, tombstones and the cracking of bullwhips. But Dylan supersedes Diddleys' Voodoo showdown with a junked up Bayou stomp that's all of his own making.

It comes crashing in from out of nowhere, taking the listener by surprise and shunting them along on an expressway into darkness. Cold black glass, brackish water that don't make no tears, fool's gold teeth, graveyard lips, nine pound hammers and steam drills, the hiss, crash and thud of slow mechanical death. But whichever Mojo Bob's got ain't working on the woman and something, she won't tell him what it is, is tearing up her mind.

Three times Dylan pleads, 'Tell me momma - What is it?' and then adds a long suffering - 'What's wrong with you this time?'

Is 'Tell Me Momma' about Edie Sedgwick and Andy Warhol? Trying to transcribe the lyrics from existing tapes is like trying to knit fog, but in the final verse the name Andy can be clearly heard in at least two versions, Manchester and Edinburgh. In the others it's a toss up between the name of Pop Art's famous founder, or, 'and he's'. By the time of the song's publication in 1971 the lyrics had been significantly altered all the way through and bear little relation to the performed work. With Edie dead could that be the reason lines were changed?

Musically, Robertson's guitar work is white hot funk, chunky and spare, reflecting Steve Cropper rather than Mike Bloomfield. This is stripped down adrenaline, demonstrating a complete understanding of the uses of an electric Fender for lead guitar playing. Robbie leads, and the rest of the band, even Dylan, follow. Thirty years later it's still a frightening opener.

Shock. Confusion. Delight. Awe.

And then - applause. Polite, perhaps a little reserved, but applause never the less.

Thoughts flew around possessed of their own mad craziness. 'Would he get rid of the band now?' - 'Would he play "Like A Rolling Stone"?' - 'Would he turn it down?'

After a short moment of tuning Dylan walked over to the microphone and spoke to us for the first time that evening. It would be an understatement to say that people hung on every word.

'This is called, "I Don't Believe You;" it used to be like that, and now it goes like this.'

A nervous ripple of laughter spread through the audience and then, before we'd barely had a chance to take in what he meant, a Cuban heeled

boot stomped the rhythm onto the floor of the Free Trade Hall and the number got under way.

I Don't Believe You

Written in 1964 and premiered on *Another Side Of Bob Dylan*, 'I Don't Believe You (She Acts Like We Never Have Met)', is a glorious free-wheeling love song with more than a hint of eroticism. Skirts sway, guitars play and mouths are watery and wet, but in the morning the woman who Dylan's spent the night with is acting like they never met. Paul Williams claims, with some justification, that in this and several other songs of the period, Dylan is celebrating an active sexuality, and it certainly comes across that way.

As an electric number it had been included in the set from as far back as August the previous year, being performed alongside 'It Ain't Me Babe' taken from the same album. Dylan risks raising the wrath of the Folk contingent but mutes it by his spoken introduction which appears to have been standard throughout the tour. Dylan and the Band then prepare to thunder their way into the tune. The reaction it gets from audiences is, initially, one of laughter.

'OK. We're hip. We've had a little laugh - now what are you going to do?'

The above unspoken follow-through is one of the key problems that we might associate with the tour - confrontation. Dylan clearly hasn't deserted his old songs, the problem lies in the fact that audiences just can't understand, or won't understand, their new settings.

The Band give the whole of 'I Don't Believe You' a solid underpinning of magisterial splendour, Robertson's sliding chords and Hudson's swirling organ rotate and interplay with the rhythm section and Dylan's harp interpolations. It works. Why don't the audience?

Dylan himself becomes physically looser during the number. He walks backwards and forwards towards Robertson, sharing the vibe that the unit as a whole is creating. Then he stalks back to the microphone again, letting go of the electric guitar long enough to press his hands to the sides of his harmonica in an indirect parody of Munch's 'The Scream'. Dylan actually looks as if he's enjoying himself, and to the Traditionalists that is possibly the greatest sin.

But, Dylan has got this far and there haven't been any of the scenes that I've been dreading. So far the audience have been polite and no one's booed. Then 'I Don't Believe You' comes to an end...

Again there's polite applause, maybe even a little warmer now that people have gotten used to the volume. On stage Rick Saunders is beginning to relax a little. The imminent attack of the brainless people hasn't materialised and Bob looks cool. The musicians begin to tune up again. Then, during the tuning up process the first protesters begin their shouting. It's faint at first, but the band pause long enough for it to gain ground and as they try to start the next number a section of the audience begins to slow hand-clap.

It is a peculiarly British way of registering displeasure, particularly at a performance. It is not a singular activity, it demands co-conspirators or fellow participants. Its ultimate message is 'Get off!' Essentially, it is 'death to the performer'. It was common in music halls as early as the previous century, but its use in a modern day concert hall was almost unthinkable. For an artist of Dylan's stature, and especially considering the sell out concerts of a year before, it was unprecedented.

The shouting, catcalling and slow hand-clapping certainly wasn't on a par with Forest Hills. Me, and others present at the concert, put the figure at around three to four dozen, though we may be wrong. Listening to the recording of that night it certainly suggests more significant numbers were involved. Lonnie recalls:

'There were about sixteen of us in the middle of the hall, but there were lots more scattered around who felt the same way we did.'

Steve Currie, who was about four rows from the front, found himself next to one of the Traditionalists:

'I wasn't too impressed by the velvet suits, but I was even less impressed by the dickhead sat next to me who decided to start booing and shouting along with the others who were scattered around the hall. I told him to fuck off home if he didn't like it. Well, that shut him up and he stayed, but the protest carried on elsewhere.'

A portion of the fracas going on, which was bound to add to the confusion of the night, was the positive response of a number of Dylan's fans. Keith Fletcher wasn't going to have his evening ruined:

'The audience politely applauded. We were still sat there in rapt attention... When the slow hand-clapping started we thought we had to stop them from doing it. When it got to a certain peak of hand-claps and boos we were shouting at them from where we were. Shouting at them to shut up. I think a lot of the noise was one lot of people telling the other lot to shut up.'

Seemingly undeterred by the noise the band played on, repeating the introductory riff to 'Baby Let Me Follow You Down.'

Baby Let Me Follow You Down

There's still a certain amount of controversy regarding who originally composed this song. On his first album Dylan, in a spoken introduction says - 'I first heard this song from Ric Von Schmidt ... Ric's a blues player ...' but the song has a history that goes far further back than that, as Ric certainly acknowledges.

The Animals, the UK R 'n' B outfit scored their first chart hit in England in March 1964 with a version called 'Baby Let Me Take You Home.' Eric Burdon claimed it was a cleaned up arrangement of an old Blues tune called 'Baby Don't You Tear My Clothes.' On their single the song-writing credit went to Russell and Farrell (which, knowing The Animals, was probably two blokes they'd met down the pub).

Robert Shelton finds links with an Alabama sharecropper called Horace Sprott who recorded for Folkways. The final word from Dylan on the song's origins is that he got it from 'Baby Let Me Lay It On You' as sung by the Reverend Gary Davis.

Whatever the song's origins, if ever there was a contender for a tune exemplifying 'Folk Rock', whatever that might be, this is it. By taking a tune with its roots firmly embedded in the American Folk tradition and then giving it an overlying rock rhythm with an electric backing, Dylan has contemporised an otherwise fixed historical moment. 'The House Of The Rising Sun,' on the other hand, also on Dylan's first album, fails to make the grade in its electric version as presented on the *Highway 61 Interactive CD*. In my view, the difference lies in the essential 'otherness' of a solid bodied electric guitar versus an acoustic. The different resonance is crucial to the song's construction. Crudely put, electric equals rock, acoustic equals ballads. The vibration and timbre is quite different in each instrument and demands a different approach in what musicians call 'attack' or 'dynamics'. Dylan has also considerably altered the harmonica part. On the acoustic version it overlays the guitar, swooping and gliding. At the Free Trade Hall it punctuates and stabs, aiding the overall rhythmic structure of the song.

Dylan harshens the delivery too. Changing it from a breathy, intimate vocal implying seduction, imploring even, to a more heightened, almost street punk 'come on'. The lyrics are broadened out as well. On the original version there's no mention of buying anyone broken spines to climb, let alone being driven out of their mind.

Perhaps the most telling lyric change (or addition), is in the final reprise where the singer offers to buy the girl a velvet skirt and a velvet shirt just so long as she won't hurt him. From a fairly obvious set of (desperate) chat up lines we've gone on to the implied success of the singer's repartee, the establishment of a relationship and the inevitability of its destruction!

'Baby Let Me Follow You Down' was premiered on October 23 1965 at the Patrick Gymnasium, University of Vermont. It signified a major change in the content of the second electric half. Both 'Maggie's Farm' and 'From A Buick Six' were dropped from the set and 'Positively Fourth Street' was also premiered. The latter number would eventually be dropped at the end of March 1966.

Dylan really let it rock on this number. His diminutive frame quivered in front of the microphone as he delivered his amended lyrics. His face took on an impish-like grimace as he alternately sang and played harmonica, occasionally bringing both his hands up to the sides of his face and looking for all the world like an even crazier version of Shakespeare's Puck girdling the Earth with his song. Bobby was boppin' and the joint was rockin'. Well, parts of it anyway. Deep within the stalls trouble was a-brewing.

After a rip-roaring final verse and coda the musicians grind to a halt and there's a split second gap before the audience start applauding. Then the shouting picks up again.

As the music crashed to another finish everybody in the hall including Dylan must have been wondering what was going to happen next. For once there wasn't going to be any tuning up between numbers. As the last chord died away and the audience started applauding, Dylan moved across to Robertson and while strumming his Fender, issued instructions. Then, almost before anybody had a chance to take a breath, and certainly before the Traditionalists had a chance to start their countermeasures, Dylan's boot heel slammed down four times, setting the beat for the opening riff of the next number.

Just Like Tom Thumb's Blues

This song made its first appearance on the *Highway 61 Revisited* album on August 30 1965. It was, and remains one of Dylan's most evocative songs, brimming with imagery, invective and a perverse beauty. It has a narrative of sorts wherein the songwriter introduces us to a group of characters that maybe, just maybe, we wouldn't want to know.

The song begins with the narrator stuck in the rain somewhere in Northern Mexico. Then he's in a bordello somewhere outside Juarez. It's Easter, which means that in a Catholic country like Mexico, the air will be laden with images of a crucified Christ and the scent of rebirth rather than tomb blood.

In the second two verses the narrator refers to two girls by name, Sweet Melinda and Saint Annie. Their names belie their intentions and maybe the song speaks more about Dylan's youthful inability to deal with female sexuality rather than the implied certainties of life that the speculative narrator mouths.

The final verse is an admission of desperation. An admission that the world is falling apart around him. The song ends with the narrator announcing that he's going back to New York City because he's had enough.

Live, the song was performed from Forest Hills onwards throughout the World Tour, proving to be a stalwart of the electric set.

Another interesting thing about this tune is the introduction that Dylan felt compelled to give it when he and The Band performed it in Melbourne. Dylan was particularly verbose that evening, and if you add all the words up here it's probably more than he says throughout the entire tour put together -

'This is about a painter down in Mexico City who travels from North Mexico up to Del Rio, Texas, all the time. His name's Tom Thumb. Right now he's about 125 years old, but he's still going. Everybody likes him a lot down there, he's got a lot of friends and er, this was when he was going through his blue period. Painting and... er, he's made countless amounts of paintings you couldn't even begin to think of. This is his blue period painting. I just dedicate this song to him. It's called "Just Like Tom Thumb's Blues".'

(From the audience a girl screams.)

'You know Tom Thumb?'

The standard 1966 concert version of 'Just Like Tom Thumb's Blues' is actually neatly subverted on the only official release of this track on the legitimate Sony/Columbia versions. Fans in Australia got it on the CD set *Masterpieces*, but those of us alive in 1966 were delivered this mega masterpiece on a vinyl platter when it was used on the B-Side of 'I Want You.' This version was from Liverpool, May 14th 1966, and contrary to all the other known recordings, legitimate or otherwise of this outstanding song, Robertson tries out a Steve Cropper-like coda riff that would defy any other version to come even close. What might at first hearing sound like a standard R 'n' B electric run, blasts into the tune and elevates it beyond funk onto a completely new plain.

I Received Your Letter Yesterday ...

Of all the strange events of that night, one particularly intrigued me. In fact I was beginning to believe that it might never have happened at all, that it had been a fantasy, when finally several of the people we interviewed confirmed that what I had seen was real and had definitely happened.

When Dylan and the Band finished 'Just Like Tom Thumb's Blues' there was polite applause and Dylan began to introduce the next number.

'This is call...' He was interrupted by a shout from the audience which broke Dylan's stride, but he carried on -

'This is called, "Yes..."'

Once again Dylan's flow was interrupted by a section of the crowd. Slow hand-clapping and footstomping punctuated by shouts, then, as suddenly as it had begun, it died down. Dylan continued for the third time to introduce the number.

'This is uh, this is called, "Yes, I See You Got Your Brand New Leopard Skin Pill Box Hat"'

Dylan dragged out every phrase and syllable of the introduction into a long drawn out, almost stoned drawl. For a moment the audience went quiet, but as the musicians began tuning up the natives got restless again and more shouting came from the barrackers.

As one of the hecklers cried out, 'Where's your silver!', a young, long-haired woman walked up the central isle to the front of the stage. Dylan stopped tuning up and bent down towards her. She reached up and passed him a note. Dylan bowed and blew her a kiss to thunderous applause from the crowd. Then he glanced at the note, put it in his pocket and turned back to the Band. The woman went back to her seat. The tuning and slow hand-clapping resumed. On the tape of the gig you can make out fragments of onstage conversation. Robertson asks Dylan:

'What's it say?' Presumably referring to the note.

Dylan replies:

'I dunno - pick it up man'

All the other bits and pieces of dialogue were drowned out by the noise that was coming from the audience. As the swell of heckling and slow hand-clapping reached a crescendo, Robbie Robertson shouted out a count in -

'One! - Two! - Three!'

CRASH!!! Into 'Leopard Skin Pill-Box Hat.'

Immediately after the gig my friend Mike and I wondered what could have been in the note? As the years passed it became an occasional memory and source of slight speculation. Some people couldn't remember the incident at all, others could, and like me wondered what the message to Dylan had been. A love letter? A petition? And then, thirty one years later, I found out.

A phone call had come through to my office as a result of an article that *The Manchester Evening News* had published asking for people who'd attended the concert to contact me. There on the other end of the line was Barbara. She explained that her daughter had shown her the article and she'd rung me up because she had been there and, more importantly, had done something that night that I might find interesting.

'And what was it?' I asked her.

'I took a note up to Dylan,' she said.

And that's how come Paul Kelly and I found ourselves in the living room of her house in an outer suburb of South Manchester listening to a tape of the concert we, Barbara and her old friend Doreen who was also with us, had been at all those years before.

They were then both in their early twenties. Doreen worked for a scientific instrument makers and by 1966 Barbara managed an office in the centre of Manchester. Dylan first came to their attention in 1965. Barbara heard him being interviewed on the 'Today' programme by Jack De Manio, on the BBC in late April .

'...And they (the BBC) were trying to say that there was some real meaning behind everything (in his songs), and he was saying there wasn't. It was just words and they just came into his mind. He wasn't thinking deeply... He made light of it and said you shouldn't be seeking any deep meaning from my words.'

Shortly after that she saw the promo clip of 'Subterranean Homesick Blues' on a Granada local magazine show, which was aired the night of his first ever appearance at the Free Trade Hall, which would date it as May 7th.

'It was something new I suppose, and it was funny. So many of his lyrics were funny. I mean, I liked the humour of it. I liked the way he spoke. It was just the whole thing altogether.'

Barbara was coming into it more from a jazz angle. That was her preferred scene. Traditional, New Orleans style jazz, but Doreen was coming at it from a slightly more contemporary angle. She'd been going to folk clubs and had already seen Joan Baez, and was the first one of the two friends to buy a Dylan album.

'It was important to me, and I liked the poetry of the words as well. I can't say why. It was almost a natural progression from folk, you know? Because we went out with people from the folk scene at the time...'

They both regarded listening to folk, or jazz as a conscious choice. Added Barbara -

'It's like, any one can listen to pop music, but in a way you choose to listen to someone like Dylan, or Leonard Cohen...'

Barbara would go round to Doreen's and together they'd listen to Dylan's first four albums.

'Doreen was keener than me I think, but I'd seen him on television. It was just growing more and more. Doreen was the one who wanted to go to the concert.'

Neither of them could remember where they had heard about Dylan's imminent appearance at the Free Trade Hall. Barbara thought it was probably from some of the younger girls at work because Dylan by then was becoming the subject of much conversation. Within one year he'd had seven chart entries into the English top twenty, and his songs were being covered by all sorts of performers ranging from Peter, Paul And Mary, to

The Byrds (who in a month's time would reach number one in the UK. On a triumphant tour they would play Manchester's Palace Theatre, where they recorded the screaming fans and later used the tape on the opening of 'So You Want To Be A Rock 'n' Roll Star?'). For better or for worse, Dylan was becoming a pop pin up.

Doreen and Barbara both remembered being really excited at the thought of finally seeing Dylan in the flesh. For a majority of people going to a concert in those days was a real event. It was a truly special occasion. Barbara and Doreen had been to clubs, they'd even been to the odd show before, but Dylan in concert was the apogee of concert-going. To many of us it was the equivalent of the second coming!

I asked Barbara and Doreen if they were aware of the controversy raging around the tour and Dylan's use of an electric backing band. Neither of them had read anything in the papers about it, but as they weren't avid readers of the music press anyway, the debate had raged around them unnoticed. They couldn't, however, have failed to notice Dylan's changing style. The first time Barbara had seen Dylan was when he was performing 'Subterranean Homesick Blues,' his infamous 'first' electric single, and she'd found it 'funny'

'I think I remember saying to you (Doreen), I hope he doesn't play any of that new stuff.'

I couldn't help but say - 'But the new stuff had been round for a year!'

'Yes,' Barbara rightly replied, 'But not on any of the albums we had!'

What Barbara and Doreen wanted to hear was the Dylan that had given them 'Love Minus Zero,' 'Don't Think Twice,' 'Ballad In Plain D,' 'Mr Tambourine Man' and 'With God On Our Side.' But most of all, it was Bob Dylan that they wanted to see...

'I thought it would be like what I'd heard on record, but seeing him live would be so much better,' recalled Barbara.

Despite all her excitement though, when Dylan actually came onstage Barbara got a shock.

'... I felt disappointed when I actually saw him. He seemed such a tiny little figure, so thin, with all that hair. He looked like a spider.... Dylan sort of crawled onto the stage.'

However, her misgivings soon gave way as Dylan ran through a string of 'standards' plus new material. Both of them thoroughly enjoyed the acoustic set and in a strange way were looking forward to the second half because they'd had such a good time during the first. I pointed out that they must have noticed the drum kit and amplifiers on the stage.

Barbara told me they had seen them. 'We did - and we were very frightened! (Laughter). He was such a diminutive figure on the stage and then all of a sudden we realized that he wasn't going to be on his own anymore...'

When Dylan and The Band started playing?

'Shock!' answered Barbara. 'Horror. I mean, first of all, we just couldn't believe the sound... It was so loud.'

Doreen added, 'It was painful... it was just pounding... I liked the acoustic things better. So it was just the worst possible thing for me. I liked the music but it just didn't sound right...'

To be fair to both Barbara and Doreen, the Free Trade Hall wasn't built for amplified music. All the people who were there that night have agreed that it was the loudest thing they'd ever heard up to that date. The acoustics in the hall were appalling. The sound we hear now on the recording of the concert is a balanced mix. The sound we heard on the night was a completely new experience to probably 99.9 per cent of us. Subjected to it you could do two things - flip or fly. Barbara and Doreen flipped.

They didn't leave though. They decided to sit the concert out. When the heckling started after 'I Don't Believe You' they began to feel distraught. When the slow hand-clapping started they felt even worse. Not for themselves but for Dylan. Recalled Barbara -

'We felt very upset for Dylan because he thinks they don't like him, but it isn't him it's The Band. That was the feeling that was going through our minds. We felt really upset for Dylan. He'd come to this country and they were treating him like this....'

Doreen added, 'When people started walking out and things were getting noisier, this is when we thought we had to do something about it...'

Now we were cutting to the chase. Thirty-one years I'd been waiting for the answer to what I knew was coming next. So I asked them, 'What did you do?'

Barbara told me, 'We wrote a note onto a scrap of paper ... Only a tatty scrap ...'

'You were rooting around in your bag to see what we could write it on.' recalled Doreen. 'We made bits of straw out of paper, and whoever drew the straw... Fortunately it was you...'

Barbara had drawn the short straw. She was the one who had to walk up to the stage and hand Dylan the note.

After all this time I was finally getting nearer.

Barbara, 'Then I walked forward ...'

Doreen, 'I thought, 'Oh God, I couldn't have done that.'

So there, on Tuesday, the 17th May 1966 at approximately nine o'clock in the evening, just after Dylan and The Band had finished 'Just Like Tom Thumb's Blues,' Barbara found herself walking up the central aisle of the Free Trade Hall towards Bob Dylan.

'I must have waited for the end of a song. I wouldn't have gone up during a number... He came forward... and I thought he was actually going to give me a kiss. Instead of that he blew me a kiss and I went "No, no. Read the note"... He did take the note... I saw him look at it and I thought, oh, he's just pretended. I don't know what he did with it, I think he put it in his pocket... I felt let down because I thought he was pretending that it was a love note... We were naive...'

Finally, I asked 'What did the note say?'

'"Tell the band to go home",' replied Barbara.

Barbara and Doreen might have been a little naive, but what they did that night was done out of the best possible intentions. They both went out of their way to assure me that at the time they thought they were doing something to protect Dylan. That he didn't realise the animosity was for the Hawks and not for him, that the sound was all wrong, that it wasn't Dylan's fault.

Unlike others they didn't boo, or walk out. After another couple of numbers they even began to get used to the sound -

'I think we got a bit more used to the noise, because we stayed. We were upset when we saw people walk out... Did he know that it was nothing to do with him personally?' said Doreen.

Sitting there in that living room, thirty-one years later, I was really impressed by the fact that these two women were prepared to tell us what had gone on that evening so long ago. At that point I hadn't managed to get anybody to admit that they'd heckled, booed or slow hand-clapped Bob. The sheer volume had phased them, but their reaction had been purely altruistic. They had wanted to save Dylan from any hurt and they truly believed that they might 'make him see sense'. Theirs had been an act of love, however misguided we might see it with hindsight, but an act of love never the less.

Everything changes and so have Barbara and Doreen over the years. As we sat and talked that night, Barbara told us how she was looking forward to seeing Dylan and Van Morrison in Manchester later in the year. We joked about whether she'd go up to the stage with a note this time round. "Sound systems are so much better now", she said. She wouldn't have to save Dylan from himself.

Leopard Skin Pill-Box Hat

This song was only five or six months old by the time Dylan reached Manchester. One of the first versions of the tune, featuring an opening riff supplied by a ringing doorbell and the musicians shouting out, 'Who's there?' had been attempted in Columbia's Studio A in New York in January 1966. That cut, however, was discarded and the song was put on hold until Dylan went to Nashville in February and recorded the version that appeared on *Blonde On Blonde*.

One of the things that singled out the released version was a credit in the liner notes that said Dylan played lead guitar on the track. This was an advancement on Dylan's 'police car' credit on *Highway 61 Revisited*. The tune, as performed on the world tour, and indeed in Manchester, always featured Robbie Robertson on lead however.

'Pill-Box' would be a simple conventional 12-bar boogie except for Dylan's enigmatic lyrics which lift it above the ordinary and into the realms of the surreal. 'Mattresses balancing on bottles of wine'? - Belts wrapped tight around Dylan's head? The implied class warfare that takes place throughout the song? The jealousy? The voyeurism? To us, stuck in Manchester in 1966, the song represented a whole new world as we listened to

it for the first time. At the side of the stage, Rick Saunders was writing down a list of numbers as Dylan played them. This was one that he wouldn't be able to place until *Blonde On Blonde* came out.

'When I heard "Leopard Skin Pill-Box Hat" I thought, "What the fuck is he going on about? Has he got a cheetah on a chain?" There was this definite feeling that that there was a big scene going on and we were only in the foothills of their heights. There we were, in the foothills watching all these wonderful people having such wonderful ideas, raising popular consciousness. It was deeply magnificent.'

'If You Only Wouldn't Clap So Hard'

There is a void at the end of 'Pill-Box Hat.' It is a void into which Chaos descends. For a brief moment confusion reigns and it seems like Dylan might actually lose the battle. Tim and Kath Green:

'The slow hand-clapping... It was terrible.... Then the shouting. I felt so embarrassed. That the people where I lived could treat him like this... It was so unfair. They'd obviously gone with the sole intention of doing it to him...'

From his position on the stage Stewart Tray must have felt that they were booing him:

'I didn't know what the hell was going on! Nasty people. I just got the feeling that there was something going on, the noise, the booing, the slow hand-clapping and all the rest of it. I mean, this was supposed to be like going to a pop concert. People threw jelly babies at pop concerts, they didn't do this kind of stuff. There was fear where I was sat that Dylan would just walk off.'

There was the same fear where I was sat, rigid and impotent in my seat, unable to quite understand why people were getting up and walking out. They did it in a very ostentatious manner by going very slowly to the front of the stage so that Dylan would see them registering their displeasure. Some of them had their hands over their ears. All that, combined with the noise they were making, made me feel that Dylan would pull out. Apparently that was the intention of those hecklers who remained. Lonnie remembers:

'I could see people walking out and I thought, "I don't blame them." The rest of us though decided to stay because we thought that we could boo him off stage, and then he did that talking bit...'

Throughout the tour during both the acoustic and electric sets Dylan very often took an inordinately long amount of time in tuning up. In Paris, a week after the Manchester concert, he was actually booed during the first half because he was taking so long to get it together. That Tuesday night in Manchester there were times when his between number routines almost took on an air of provocation. Rick Saunders:

'I think the long tune-ups were [an act of] defiance. Very calculated. He was such a cool guy. Whatever he was on had him operating on a very different velocity to anyone else, even the band, and they were his cohorts.'

Keith Fletcher felt the same -

'Long, long re-tunings, and stumbling about and getting water and harmonicas, and talking to the band. That led to a lot of the booing inbetween numbers, the delays. In a way he seemed to be encouraging the slow hand-clapping... '

Perhaps Dylan needed to feed off that negative energy being thrown at him by the crowd? With reflection and hindsight it does appear to have been an act of incredible masochism, this nightly ritual of humiliation and pain. But these are the very things that drive the music along, creating the unique power of those electric performances. Maybe Dylan needed the confrontational adrenaline? Kept jacking it in like a gigantic syringe stuck straight into his heart. A man mainlining hatred directly into his veins for a buzz that none of us will ever know? What other possible earthly reason could there be for going through with it day after day, country after country?

Just when the madness seemed to be getting totally out of hand Dylan performed a trick that switched the whole situation round. In order to get the audience's attention he began to mumble quietly into the microphone. Just little bits of nonsense, fragments of no-sense, that could, maybe, if you could hear it properly, have made some sense. Invariably the crowd will quieten down long enough to listen. When the booing and stomping had stopped Dylan moved in with the punchline - 'If you only wouldn't clap so hard'. Momentarily taken aback the audience laughed at Dylan's sardonic humour. It was an old carnival barker's routine, but it worked its magic on the crowd. And, it was something Dylan had used before.

The previous night at the Gaumont in Sheffield Dylan had faced a similarly hostile crowd and went into the mumbling routine. The crowd duly calmed down and Dylan finished off the rambling monologue with the following coherent sentences -

'I was just a baby - Remember, I was a baby once'.

Again they laughed at the absurdity of Dylan's statement, and for a brief second he had the audience back on his side.

What is of significance isn't that Dylan had used the routine more than once, but the point within the concert where he played out this particular act of the psychodrama. On both recorded occasions it came between 'Leopard Skin Pill-Box Hat' and 'One Too Many Mornings.' If there is any truth in the argument that Dylan and Grossman orchestrated the mania of those nights then this coincidence lends weight to the theory. I don't suggest that there was a deliberate policy to offend, the Fender alone would provide that without any other machinations on Dylan's part, but, as I've stated above, perhaps there existed on Dylan's part a subconscious desire for confrontation - to face the enemy head on.

Whatever the design, the effect was achieved and so, to cheers and applause, Dylan kicked off into one of his most personal songs. One that had appeared in his repertoire long before 1966 and would continue to do so long after.

One Too Many Mornings

Here Dylan presents us with a snapshot of a young man trying to come to terms with a broken love affair. Robert Shelton states (probably with some authority) that it was written about Suze Rotolo and Dylan's doomed relationship. From the opening line we're immediately drawn into the singer's world of hurt. You can imagine him walking the streets, his physical body aware of the night falling, but his mind being inexorably drawn back again and again to his lost love.

The singer is tortured and plagued by the thoughts inside his mind. He cannot find any peace and no matter where he is, spiritually he keeps being drawn back to the relationship.

Slowly, a Zen-like realisation overtakes him and he begins to see with a clarity which he has been denying himself. There are no arguments because there can be no victor. Both of them are as vanquished as their love now is, because, 'You're right from your side and I am right from mine'. Here he acknowledges the futility of rationalisation within the framework of the heartland and its workings. Lovesickness conquers logic and they're 'both one too many mornings and a thousand miles behind'.

On the *The Times They Are A Changing* album where the song first appeared, 'Mornings' is a gentle, lilting ballad, almost whispered and certainly tender. The three verses (unusual for Dylan to practice such economy) are punctuated by quiet, lyrical passages on the harmonica. The electric version, however, is heavy.

In *The Yellow Emperor's Book Of Medicine*, a thousand year old Taoist Chinese treatise, the elements have a variety of attributes depending on the physician's prognosis and the state of the patient's Chi, or life-forces. One of the elements in Taoist medicine is Metal, and the sound of Metal is weeping. The electric version of 'Mornings' to me too is the sound of Metal weeping. It seeps through every note and cascades downwards onto the stage floor. The notes from Robertson's solo are like drops of mercury showering off the strings: teardrops made of lead.

The descending patterns of the bass riff are made of solid iron. As the hook phrase is reached at the end of every verse Rick Danko plays two notes which bring him up to the microphone to sing the word 'Be - hind!' in harmony with Dylan. He then steps back and the streams of Metal continue to pour out into the night.

At the end of the number the booing is more muted than before. Maybe Dylan was wearing them down with his tenacity? The slow hand-clapping sounds quieter too. The odd shout comes from out of the stalls, but basically, at this point we realised that Dylan wasn't going to give up. The stage was incandescent with energy.

Ballad Of A Thin Man

Dylan took off his guitar and placed it next to his amplifier and moved across the stage to the piano which Richard Manuel was just vacating. Dylan sat down, highlighted in a single spot and immediately began the opening riff of 'Thin Man.'

Repeatedly throughout the tour Dylan fended off questions about 'Protest' songs and such like. Again and again, he denied that any of his songs had messages, and yet it is clear that Dylan was often being disingenuous. And, if any of his songs ever had a message this was the one. It's a song about cool, about hip versus un-hip. It's directed at those in the know about those who don't. It's an in-joke and it's an attack on the sensibilities of some one who won't even realise what the song is about. That the line, 'You know something is happening but you don't know what it is, do you Mr Jones?', has now entered the lexicon of popular usage, is evidence enough that this scathing epistle was certainly understood by many.

In the mid-sixties Dylan was the epitome of hip: he oozed cool from every pore in his body. The enigmatic liner notes and photographs. The fact that so little information about the man was ever forthcoming. The Beatles were too cuddly ever to be totally hip, the Stones too obviously trying for hipdom. Only Dylan was ever truly, solidly, honest to goodness, laid-down, freaky hip. The Raybans, the giant lightbulb, the ever-present cigarette, the curled lip and the putdown, all denoted a man seriously intent on being cool. Dylan couldn't have been square if he'd tried. Even when he cut off his hair it was hip. And here, now, for those of us pathetic people who hoped one day to be slightly, remotely as hip as Bob, was a manual of put-downs. This handbook, made explicitly for storage and retrieval at appropriate moments when the occasion demanded. Dylan's words, those fabulously scintillating bon-mots, could be pulled out from the data bank and put to effective use any good time.

That night in the Free Trade Hall the guitar and piano sent out that repeated pattern, those descending minor chords, and a shiver went up and down the spine. It was a frightening sound, bordering on psychedelia, or possibly clinical schizophrenia. Garth Hudson on the organ was making swirling and demonic music from The Circus Of Death. Hudson trills and thrills up and down the keyboard as Dylan barrages the hapless Mr Jones with his caustic put downs and buckets of pith, while the rest of the band get to kick ass too as the tune thunders through its progressions and changes. 'Ballad Of A Thin Man' is conceit, bravado and genius transmuted into one of the great tunes of the 20th century.

Judas!

Having delivered the message of 'Thin Man,' Dylan got up from his piano stool, bowed to the applauding members of the audience and strolled back to put on his guitar and harmonica. As he checked his harmonica tuning one of the most (in)famous shouts in Rock 'n' Roll history came shrieking out from somewhere near the middle of the stalls.

'Judas!'

Lonnie, can't put a name to the voice -

'It actually wasn't one of us. It came from just over on my left and I thought, 'Great!' and started applauding.'

And applaud the Judas-shouter the Traditionalists did. Just when we thought they'd all finished, dried up, been defeated, the heckling started once more. Only this time, if such a thing were possible, the chosen cry was one of insanity at fever pitch.

151

There can be few people by 1966 who weren't aware that Dylan was a Jew. Up until the year before, within the Christian world, Jews were still officially regarded as being responsible for the death of Jesus of Nazareth. Only 21 years before, this had been one of the excuses used for the extermination of Jews in Europe. Millions of Dylan's blood-kin had been massacred in an act of genocide, the likes of which the world had never seen before. In 1965 Pope John XXIII had graciously exonerated the Jewish people from all blame in a Papal encyclical, but anti-semitism still had a presence in Europe. In Britian, Neo-Nazi groups such as The National Front were re-emerging from their sewers. In America, Dylan had already lampooned George Lincoln Rockwell, leader of the American Nazi Party, in a talking blues. To shout 'Judas' at a Jew in 1966 was an act of mind-boggling stupidity and senselessness.

I don't think for one minute that the perpetrator of the insult had any concept of the racial loading in the word that he had hurled at Dylan. What he had in mind was merely to accuse Dylan of selling out the cause of Traditional Folk Music, and certainly he couldn't have realised on the night that his accusatory outcry would continue to ring throughout the decades. And though many people are intrigued by his identity, it's difficult to imagine anyone coming forward and admitting to it now, and, even so, I feel that the act of oral violence he carried out should be enough to deny him even a second's worth of fame.

Consider the people D.A. Pennebaker filmed in the foyer of the Free Trade Hall after the show. People, all good citizens of a town called Malice, who said that Dylan should, 'Be shot. He's a traitor.' 'Pop groups sing better rubbish than he does.' Look at them and gaze in wonder. You would have thought that Dylan, Robertson, et al, had rode into town on coal black steeds and slaughtered their first born, raped their virgins and spat on their grandmothers. All he did was to sing a few songs, but to these people Dylan was the essence of the Anti-Christ. The reaction of the Traditionalists against one man who chose to do what he wanted to do speaks volumes.

Lonnie is still bitter to this day, but he sees no dichotomy in the reception he and his friends gave Dylan in Manchester.

'It was like, as if, everything that we held dear had been betrayed. He showed us what to think, though I know that's a stupid thing to say. But there he was, marching with Martin Luther King and everything, and suddenly he was singing this stuff about himself. We made him and he betrayed the cause.'

'We waited, and then out came *Blonde On Blonde*. We waited then out came all the other albums. It wasn't until 'George Jackson' that I thought, "Hey, hang on here. He's finally seen sense." And then.... Crap, just crap.'

As if stunned by the heckler's scream, Dylan and the band carried on tuning up. Another idiot shouted out, this time from further away:

'Do a solo!!'

Time stands still, and Dylan hasn't heard this one. In his mind he's still thinking over the crap that he's had from the guy before.

'Judas!'

It appears to echo through Dylan's mind. He stalks over to Robertson who's looking protectively over at his gear. 'Maybe Bob's gone too far this time?'

Dylan glances around at the other musicians. Mickey Jones, connoisseur of fine Nazi regalia looks down at Dylan, sticks at the ready. Mickey, fine old Mickey, has no idea of the brouhaha the gig has caused. Working Vegas with Trini was never like this.

Manuel, now restored to his place at the keyboards, is in a world of his own, as is Danko. Hudson, however, glares over his organ at Bob, grinning and ready to take it from whatever parameter of hell that Dylan decides to call upon. Hudson is a Gonzo organ player and twice as ready to shoot from the hip as the others give him credit for. But Dylan's been thinking about the heckler and what his message imparts. He strides up to the microphone.

Like A Rolling Stone

'I don't believe you'.

Everybody on stage has now picked up the riff and the adrenaline. This is full-steam ahead, no quarter asked and no quarter given.

From our seats around the hall we were as excited as we could be. We could hear the riff. It was the idiot bastard son of 'La Bamba,' or 'Twist &

Shout,' or whatever else we wanted it to be. For Kevin Fletcher, Steve Currie, or all the rest of us that were there, 'Like A Rolling Stone' was the one we'd waited nearly a year for. But Bob wasn't finished yet. Once again he walked up to the microphone,

'You're a liar.'

The opening riff from 'Like A Rolling Stone' continued, relentlessly in the background. Somebody, it may be Dylan or it may be Robertson continues -

'Get (or, 'Play', or, 'You're a fuckin' liar.') fucking loud!'

With a crash on the cymbals, Mickey Jones vents all the pent up anger, agony and frustration in a barrage of passion and intensity. It is a great release. It's like somebody with toothache has been given a free hit of apomorphine and feels the pain draining away. For a brief moment this is Mickey's song.

Because this is the greatest of Bob Dylan's songs to boot and here he is, prepared to sing it ... despite the noises to the contrary.

And so it should be because this is the country where the song had its genesis. You can see the seeds laid down in *Don't Look Back*, where Dylan is at the piano.

'Sing Hank William's "Lonesome Highway",' shouts Bobby Neuwirth. Dylan does and in the chords we can hear echoes of whatever was to come to fruition in the month or so ahead.

Now, this may or not be another song about Edie Sedgwick, but to us, in Manchester in 1966, it was a clarion call. A battlecry for Freedom. We didn't know the ins and outs of the New York Glitteratti's love affairs. We knew little of contemporary Popular Culture, except for the dribs and drabs that were spoon fed to us via the medium of the Sunday broadsheet colour supplements. Suddenly, here was Dylan, offering us a view of the Socialite life of the Big Apple, that we wouldn't have known much about anyway, but still, thank you Bob for offering it. And even if we knew nothing about nothing, still we had nothing to lose - we were invisible then, and only Dylan seemed to care.

I think I knew, way back in 1965, when I first heard this single, that this was the one. This would be the song that if ever I heard it, on the radio or the TV, or whatever, I would say - 'Yes, they're playing my tune'. 'Like

A Rolling Stone' inspired a generation, and, you can try, as an experiment, the following question:

'Where were you when you first heard Dylan's 'Rolling Stone?'

No matter what the variety of answers that you get, the thing is that people remember the first time they heard it. In musical terms it was the end of the world, and the beginning. At that point in the 20th century, your reaction to the first time that you heard 'Rolling Stone' showed whether you were on the bus or under it. It was as simple as that.

Now here we were, in the presence of the creator of THAT song. And it was THAT song that we were waiting to hear. Jones came first with his cymbal crash and the opening lyric of 'Once upon a time you dressed so fine ...'

Keith Fletcher:

'A live version of "Like A Rolling Stone"! You know as well as I do that live versions don't match the quality of studio version. Well, this captured the studio version but it was much more enhanced. I was just knocked out by it. I was amazed.'

Steve Currie:

'It's what I was waiting to hear.'

Paul Kelly:

'I could hardly hold my camera in excitement. This was it. "Like A Rolling Stone"!'

'Like A Rolling Stone' was the valiant last stand of the Dylan brigade. This was to be Bob's Battle of the Little Big Horn. Still his cavalry came crashing on in the form of Mickey Jones and the rest of the band.

As Dylan snarled his way through the opening riff it became clear that this was it. This was to be the final part of a titanic struggle that wrought apart the minds and reasoning of a generation of young people. In a sense it demanded that you came down for the cause of Modernism, or stood aside for the cause of.... What? We didn't know. Perhaps it would be left up to the Traditionalists who had booed and slow hand-clapped their way through Dylan's set to show the way forward, but in reality, even then it was obvious that it wasn't to be them.

In 1966, for the majority of us Dylan offered an alternative to our day to day existence that was exemplified by the lyrics of all the songs he sang to us that night. It was the culmination of a four-year journey for Bob not to be identified as a Messiah or a Guru, or, even as a Folk singer. Just simply as a person who had a tale to tell, or a song to sing. Songs that, though they appeared to be packed with meaning, as they truly were, they had but one lesson to offer us - and that lesson was that we were to think for ourselves, not rely on leaders or savants, no matter how cool they appeared.

The principal lesson to be learned from studying the lyrics of 'Like A Rolling Stone' was so simple - 'How does it feel - To be on your own?'.

And that summed us up - the lost, the hopeful, the lonely, the obsessed, but all of us there on the evening of the 17th May 1966 hoping to get a glimpse of a young American who for whatever reason summed up our dreams, aspirations and, occasionally nightmares too.

No one booed at the end of the concert when Dylan finished spitting and cursing his way through 'Like A Rolling Stone.' The man himself stood rigidly at the microphone and announced a curt 'Thank you', before rushing off the stage.

Aftermath

From his vantage point at the side of the stage door Malcolm Metcalfe was swept up in the confusion:

'... we weren't sure if it had ended because there was this sudden silence and the doors blasted open and Dylan and some heavies rushed past us and I remember thinking, "My God, he's so small!" And we followed them down the corridor and they jumped into this big, black limousine and they were away ...'

Inside the hall confusion also reigned. The intensity of the performance of 'Like A Rolling Stone' left the majority of the audience breathless and dumbfounded. As the final chord was fading away cheers mixed in with the applause. There were very few, if any boos. Some people shouted for more, but clearly it was over. Dylan had given of his all and there was no more left. I remember thinking maybe he would come back on, but after the reception he'd been given that seemed a futile fantasy. I just didn't want him to go away. I stood up and looked around at others doing the same thing. Wondering, what to do? What to do?

People were heading towards the exits and back into the foyer, but not all of them. Rick Saunders was guarding the stage.

'I stayed there right through to the finish and people were coming up and demanding their money back, thinking that somehow I'd be able to give it to them, but the whole thing was finished....'

Tim and Kath couldn't move from their seats they were so transfixed by the performance:

'A lot of people had left immediately... a lot of people had walked out during the set... We sat there for quite a while... just sat there.'

Paul Kelly and his friends had been watching a group of Americans at the foot of the stage. The Americans were fiddling with a large reel to reel tape recorder:

'We just went up to them you know. And we were talking to them and I asked if we could have a copy of the tape. I don't know what we would have played it on! Anyway, they were quite polite and friendly but it was obvious we couldn't have a copy so we made our way out.'

In the foyer people milled around still stunned, excited or outraged by what they'd just seen. The atmosphere was electric and abuzz with conversation. D.A. Pennebaker was filming interviews with members of the crowd that would later appear in *Eat The Document*. Neville, who two years before had looked after Dylan at the ABC TV studios is one of them.

'I thought he was great man, yeah. A little bit over amplified in the second half, but still ...'

Others were less generous, seemingly filled with a physical hatred and loathing for Dylan and his new music. Now, over thirty years later, it makes compulsive viewing. How could any body be so bitter? How could anybody have not been impressed by what they'd seen and heard?

States Lonnie, still unrepentant after all these years.

'I look back on it as the great lost opportunity. He could have moved the world and he just wanted to make money. There's nothing wrong with earning a living, but he went too far and sold out the people who made him.'

Lonnie is in the background of one of D.A.'s interviews.

It didn't take long for those of us who were there to realise that we had attended something that was both magnificent and historical. Something that would stay with us for the rest of our lives -

'It was one of those events that if you were at it, it changed your life.'

'That's the time in my life when I started to become an adult.'

'It affected me permanently. I was just elated. It's there forever. It was the greatest concert that I've ever been to. It shaped a whole lot of things for me. I've never ever looked back...'

'I just didn't understand this Folk versus Pop thing. I loved *Bringing It All Back Home*. I just couldn't understand all the booing... I still get very emotional when I talk about it because Dylan did literally change my life. He taught me so much...'

Coda

The punishing, gruelling tour wasn't over yet. On the 18th or 19th of May, Dylan headed North to Scotland and faced the same barrage of insults in Glasgow and Edinburgh. Then it was down to Newcastle and then off to Paris.

He played at the Olympia on May 24th, his birthday. He was stoned or drunk, or both, and the reception was again hostile.

The tour ended at the Royal Albert Hall where Dylan played for two consecutive nights.

After a short holiday in Spain with Sarah, Dylan returned to the States and began work on editing *Eat The Document* for a one hour TV special, finalising arrangements for the publication of *Tarantula*, and making preparations for a 64 date US tour scheduled to begin in August.

On July 29th, Dylan fell off his motorcycle and broke his neck. It was a crash that probably saved his life.

'That was a brush, I survived that, but what I survived after that was even harder to survive than the motorcycle crash. That was just a physical crash, but sometimes in life there are things you cannot see, that are harder to survive than something which you can pin down.'

Bob Dylan, *Playboy* magazine, 1978.

Notes

CHAPTER ONE

First Time Around

I reconstructed the events that took place on that particular day in May 1964 from information given to me by the principal witness, Neville Kellett, as well as from accounts of other people who worked at the studio at that time, and from listening to an audio recording made during the show. Obviously it is not a verbatim account and after such a great distance in time, memories can be shaky, recollections flawed or soured by subsequent events. Nonetheless, I chose to write it this way because I felt that it might give the reader a feeling for the flavour of the time and a sense of immediacy.

For background material I delved into the archives of the *TV Times* and *The Manchester Evening News*. The information pertaining to Didsbury I know at first hand having been born there in 1950, and having lived there until 1968.

For the idea to present the piece in the present tense, I gratefully acknowledge the inspiration given to me by the opening chapters of Ross Russell's *Bird Lives - The Charlie Parker Story* and *Ladies and Gentlemen - Lenny Bruce* by Albert Goldman.

CHAPTER TWO

It Could Even Be Like A Myth

As regards the influence of the CPGB on Dylan gigs, journalist/photographer Bleddyn Butcher gave me this interesting little anecdote:

A former member of the Communist Party of Scotland told Bleddyn that before Dylan's appearances in Glasgow and Edinburgh in 1966 the party cadre held a meeting. The purpose of this gathering was to decide how to best demonstrate their feelings about the direction that Dylan's music had gone in. After much heated debate it was decided to buy tickets and attend the shows. If Dylan persisted in his madness of using an electric backing group positive action would have to be taken to point out to him the error of his ways. A vote was then taken on how best to protest. Slow hand clapping followed by a walk out was decided on as the best way of registering their displeasure. This they duly did.

As Dylan told Ralph J Gleason just before the tour reached Europe – 'You can't tell where the booing's going to come up. Can't tell at all. It comes up in the weirdest, strangest places and they do it in blocks and when it comes it's a thing in itself. I mean they must be pretty rich to be able to go someplace and boo. I couldn't afford it if I were in their shoes.'

For anybody interested in pursuing this period of history further the following books, from which I drew source material for this chapter, would be worthy of investigation:

Georgina Boyes, *The Imagined Village*.

Robin Denselow, *When The Music's Over*.

Dave Harker, *Fakesong*.

George Melly, *Owning Up*.

Anthony Scaduto, *Bob Dylan*.

Robert Shelton, *No Direction Home*.

CHAPTER THREE

Mixed Up Confusion

For the opening sections, have drawn on my own experiences of being on the road with a band for sustained periods. The factual information relating to Dylan's World tour has been drawn from a wide variety of sources, including -

Craig McGregor, *Bob Dylan: A Retrospective*, biographies by Scaduto and Shelton, and Daniel Kramer's, *Bob Dylan*. (A fine photo journalistic appraisal, and a book Bob is alleged to have tried to get banned.)

The quotes from Joe Boyd are taken from an inteview conducted by Jonathon Morley that appeared in *The Telegraph*, No 37.

An invaluable look at the Cambridge Folk scene, circa 1959 to 1967, is contained in *Baby Let Me Follow You Down* by Ric Von Schmidt and Jim Rooney.

Further information for this chapter came from e-mail correspondence with Al Kooper.

Additional material appertaining to Newport can be gleaned from Greil Marcus, *Invisible Republic*, Picador, 1997, and for information on recording sessions that were taking place at the time there's Clinton Heylin, *Dylan - Behind Closed Doors* and Paul Williams, *Bob Dylan - Performing Artist - 1960-1973*.

CHAPTER FOUR

Outlaw Blues

The account of Forest Hills is drawn from reminiscences in Kramer, Shelton, Scaduto, McGregor and Marcus. Clinton Heylin's *Bob Dylan - Day By Day - 1941-1993 - A Life In Stolen Moments*, has also been of invaluable help in piecing together Dylan's hectic schedule. Plus, thanks go again to Al Kooper. The late John Bauldie's privately issued book *The Ghost Of Electricity* was an extremely useful source for contemporary news clippings.

I was also greatly helped by having an audience tape of the gig, which, though of fairly poor quality, does capture the atmosphere of that chilly August night. The taper was obviously positioned within a group of 'protesters' and their howling occasionally dominates the soundtrack.

Tapes exist of the Melbourne concert. They were taken from Australian TV and radio and are of excellent quality. For a first hand account I am very grateful to Tricia Jungwirth. For further information on the Australian leg of the tour, visit Tricia's Web site -

http://www.geocities.com/Heartland/Hills/5581/

CHAPTER FIVE

The Geography Of Innocence

Compiling a short history of key points in the history of Manchester was greatly facilitated by the archives of the Manchester Area Psychogeographic, a defunct Situationist group. Information was also derived from Michael Kennedy's long out of print Portrait of Manchester, and a neat little tome published by The Camden Society in 1883, entitled, *The Private Diary of Dr John Dee. A Facsimile of the Original MS* in the Ashmolean Museum.

Positioning the concert in its own socio-historical context was the result of a search through back issues of *The Manchester Evening News*. I drew from my own memory and from information given in interviews with the following people who were at the Free Trade Hall that night -

Dave Rothwell, Malcolm Metcalfe, Tim and Kath Green, Stewart Tray, Paul Kelly, Steve Currie, Kevin Fletcher.

CHAPTER SIX

Mr Tambourine Man

The shenanigans with the road crew and sound recordists at the Free Trade Hall are drawn from the recollections of a member of staff who worked as a porter throughout the 1960s and 1970's, and conversations with a former manager of the Free Trade Hall. The letter to Tito Burns signed 'A.S.' is presumably from the General Manager and is held in the Manchester City Archives.

The section pertaining to the IBC and Pennebaker recordings of the gig draws from an interesting article by Roger Ford in *Isis* Magazine Number 73. Dylan's 'Drug' speech is taken from *Melody Maker*, first week of June 1966 issue.

Recordings of the concert are available in a variety of formats and are outlined in the Appendices section of this book.

Memories of the night's events are from interviews with Rick Saunders, Dave Rothwell, Paul Kelly, Roger and Jane Harvey, Stewart Tray, Kevin Fletcher, Tim and Kath Green, Steve Currie, Malcolm Metcalfe, Barbara Murray and Doreen McGee, Neville Kellett, Lonnie 'X' and my own memories.

For inspiration and information in recounting and analysing the songs in the first half of the set I found the following volumes particularly illuminating:

Concerning recording and discographical matters, Heylin's *Behind Closed Doors* proved as ever invaluable.

Paul William's *Bob Dylan - Performing Artist - 1960 - 73*, provided some interesting ideas and insights into Dylan analysis. As did Shelton and Scaduto.

The occult reading of She Belongs To Me was ably assisted by EE Rhemus's *The Magician's Dictionary*, with further information from Shelton.

John Lennon's 'fascination' with Bob Dylan is covered in Ray Coleman's essential biography, *John Lennon*.

CHAPTER SEVEN

How Does It Feel?

For how it felt to be there that night during the second half I've used my own recollections plus the interviews that I conucted with Paul Kelly, Steve Currie, Tim and Kath Green, Barbara Murray, Doreen McGee, Kevin Fletcher, Lonnie 'X', Stewart Tray, Rick Saunders, Malcolm Metcalfe, and Roger and Jane Harvey.

For information about original recording dates and performance dates once again Clinton Heylin and *Day By Day* and *Behind Closed Doors* have been invaluable.

For information pertaining to specific songs I have drawn on material from Victor Bockris's Warhol, Paul Williams, Shelton, Scaduto, and Marcus.

For those of you with a multi-media inclination, Columbia and Graphic Zone's *Highway 61 CD Rom* has much interesting and useful information regarding recordings and sessions, including much rare and unique material such as a Dylan electric version of 'House Of The Rising Sun'.

Plus, of course, the whole gamut of bootleg recordings of the gig that are outlined in the discography.

Finally, the whole atmosphere of the electric set is (im)perfectly captured on the anti-documentary, *Eat The Document*.

BIBLIOGRAPHY

The following books were used as primary and secondary sources and are whole-heartedly recommended to the casual or ardent visitor to this volume.

Bauldie, John, *The Ghost Of Electricity*, privately published 1988.

Bauldie, John, (Ed), *Wanted Man - In Search Of Bob Dylan*, Citadel, 1991.

Becker, H.S. (Eds), *The Other Side: Perspectives on Deviance*, Berkeley Free Press 1963.

Bockris, Victor, *Warhol*, Penguin, 1990.

Boyes, Georgina, *The Imagined Village*, The Manchester University Press, 1993.

Chambers, Tim, *Popular Culture - The Metropolitan Experience*, Routledge 1986.

Coleman, Ray, *John Lennon*, MacMillan, (Reissued) 1997.

Copper, Bob, *A Song For All Seasons*, William Heinemann Ltd, 1971.

Crowe, Cameron, *Biograph*, booklet included with boxed set, CBS, 1986.

Crowley, Aleister, *777*, Samuel Weiser Inc, 1973.

Davis, Miles, *Miles - The Autobiography*, Touchstone, New York, 1989.

Dee, John, *Diary Of Dr John Dee*, The Camden Society, 1883.

Denselow, Robin, *When The Music's Over*, Faber & Faber, 1989.

Deren, Maya, *Divine Horsemen*, Thames & Hudson, 1953.

Goodman, Fred, *Mansion On The Hill*, Random House, 1997.

Helm, Levon, *This Wheel's On Fire*, Plexus, 1994

Heylin, Clinton, *Bob Dylan - A Life In Stolen Moments*, Book Sales Ltd, 1996.

Heylin, Clinton, *Dylan Behind Closed Doors*, St Martin's Press, 1995.

Heylin, Clinton, *Great White Wonders*, Viking, 1994.

Hoskyns, Barney, *Across The Great Divide: The Band And America*, Viking, 1993

Kennedy, Michael, *A Portrait Of Manchester*, Robert Hale, 1970.

Kooper, Al, *Backstage Passes*, Stern and Day, 1977

Kramer, Daniel, *Bob Dylan*, Citadel, 1967.

Lee, CP, *Popular Music In Manchester - 1955 - 1995*. PhD Thesis, Institute of Popular Culture, Manchester Metropolitan University, 1997.

Marcus, Greil, *Invisible Republic*, Macmillan, 1997.

McGregor, Craig, *Bob Dylan - A Retrospective*, William Morrow & Company Inc, 1972.

Rhemus, EE, *The Magician's Dictionary*, Feral House, 1990.

Scaduto, Anthony, *Bob Dylan - An Intimate Biography*, (reissued) Helter Skelter Publishing, 1996.

Shelton, Robert, *No Direction Home*, William Morrow & Company Inc, 1986.

Von Schmidt, Eric & Rooney, Jim, *Baby Let Me Follow You Down*, Anchor Press, 1989.

Ward, Ed, *Michael Bloomfield: The Rise And Fall Of An American Guitar Hero*, Cherry Lane Books, 1983.

Williams, Paul, *Performing Artist Vol 1 - 1960 - 1973*, Underwood Miller, 1990.

Magazines & Publications

On The Tracks (USA)

Isis (UK)

Dignity (UK)

APPENDIX ONE
Eat The Document

In early 1966 Albert Grossman negotiated a deal with America's ABC Television for a one hour long documentary to be shown in the new Fall season as part of the 'Stage 67' series. It was decided to use the tour as the basis for the TV special and D.A. Pennebaker who had already shot Dylan's *Don't Look Back* was hired to film the European leg of the tour, starting in Copenhagen on April 30th.

The resulting film, edited by Dylan and Howard Alk, was rejected by ABC executives who found its complete lack of narrative and its unconventional format 'unwatchable'. It has rarely been seen in public though it is of course available as a bootleg, usually in poor quality.

Take One

Motion: the whole film is about motion and motion implies speed. And speed implies the 1966 tour. Throughout the movie we constantly see, or are inside, planes, trains and automobiles. There is no stasis; wheels are constantly turning and people constantly moving. The camera too is constantly in motion. Scenes come and go for no apparent reason. Sometimes they reappear, often they do not. We get fragments of tunes, fragments of spaces, snatches of dialogue that border on the obscure and the obtuse. What we also get is a cinematic representation of where Dylan's head was at in 1966.

The film opens on a simple title shot. The words 'Eat The Document' in white on a red background. Apparently, the title was suggested by Al Aronowitz, Rock critic and an early Dylan landlord. In *Who Threw The Glass Magazine*, D.A. Pennebaker recalled, 'It was like 'eat shit' which was fine'

On the whole *Don't Look Back* is infinitely more satisfying in terms of it being a 'well made' movie, but *Eat The Document* has its own charm and style. Even though Dylan and Alk edited it, they can't get away from the fact that it was shot by one of the best cinema verite stylists of this century, D.A. Pennebaker. Strip away the 'speed' footage of sheep, exteriors of the Albert Hall, dachsunds being led across zebra crossings, etc, and the rest of the shots point to a creative artist who knows intuitively where he is pointing the camera. The Free Trade Hall sequences are particularly telling in their representation of madness (from the audience angle that is), but the best bits are of course the concert footage. Here Pennebaker shines with his own particular brilliance. The 'Thin Man' footage alone, which has been shown in its entirety on the BBC series 'Dancing In The Street' is worth the price of admission.

Pennebaker in *WTHGM* again: 'Yeah, that's a fantastic shot isn't it? You know, that was a home made lens, I made that lens. There was no lens like that then, it made marvellous distortions. I love it, the light would flare out.'

For me the film works. It probably does for most Dylan fans because it is a document of a specific time in his career, and also it is an actual statement within documentary film making. Left to a professional editor we would have got a reasonable documentary. Left to Dylan we have been given an anti-documentary that raises as many questions as it provides answers. One can see why the TV executives way back in the 1960s were horrified/terrified of *Eat The Document*: it is awkward and occasionally maladroit. It is the first attempt by somebody unschooled in film making to attempt to put together a coherent piece, whilst wishing at the same time to be fresh and original. And ... with the best will in the world, as a film, it hasn't worked. Nonetheless, for all its perceived flaws, *Eat The Document* is a unique travelogue into the inner mind of an artist at the peak of his powers, and captures his perceptions of what was going on around him at the time, in a way that representations in other media have failed. What is sad, is that Dylan won't allow the film to go on general release, even now at the threshold of a new millennium and a period of reappraisal of his entire canon.

On reflection though, perhaps this is a film that is best served by its unavailability? If it had come out in the 1960s when it was scheduled to, *Eat The Document* would have resulted in the same kind of critical drubbing to that received by The Beatles for *Magical Mystery Tour.* And, like that film it is probably too much of its time. Better maybe to leave it with its own mystique untouched. Now, as then, critics and society don't like artists mixing their media. It leads to too much confusion.

APPENDIX 2
Discography

One of the problems associated with trying to compile a complete discography of the period covered in this book is the fact that the world of the bootleg and even of the official releases is continually changing. However, here is an honest attempt to keep the lists as up to date as is possible as of January 1998.

Again, it is worth pointing out that bootleg recordings are illegal in many parts of the world, including the United Kingdom.

Essentially, the set that Dylan and The Hawks performed throughout the 1966 World Tour never strayed from the following:

ACOUSTIC SET

She Belongs To Me, Fourth Time Around, Visions Of Johanna, It's All Over Now, Baby Blue, Desolation Row, Just Like A Woman, Mr Tambourine Man

ELECTRIC SET

Tell Me Mamma, I Don't Believe You, Baby Let Me Follow You Down, Just Like Tom Thumb's Blues, Leopard Skin Pill-Box Hat, One Too Many Mornings, Ballad Of A Thin Man, Like A Rolling Stone

The first release pertaining to the whole electric shebang was the B-Side of 'I Want You' in 1966. This was a fairly startling live version of 'Just Like Tom Thumb's Blues' recorded in Liverpool on May 19th 1966. The performance itself is rather dynamic featuring a different coda than the rest of the recordings I've heard from the tour. For some years this was the only evidence that we had that the tour had actually taken place, if you understand what I mean? Here it was: a document of an irreplaceable fragment of reality preserved forever on vinyl, the Band cutting up a storm as Dylan ranted on about life in Juarez. It was poetic and frightening at the same time. After its release as the B-Side of the single the recording slipped into obscurity until it was included on a CD entitled *Masterpieces*. Unfortunately this is only available in Australia, or on import in the UK.

Another example of Dylan and The Hawks playing live on the tour then surfaced on the *Biograph* boxed set. This was 'I Don't Believe You,' originally attributed to Belfast on May 6th, but actually taken from Dublin the day before. Not quite one of the best, but as a representation of the overall sound, not too bad either.

Acoustic cuts have also appeared in legitimate form. 'It's All Over Now Baby Blue' taken from Manchester on May 17th can be heard on *Biograph*, as can 'Visions Of Johanna' which is from the Albert Hall on May 26th

In terms of what is available in bootleg form the ground becomes murkier, but accessible never the less. Firstly here's a list of the currently available bootleg

CDs, courtesy of John Howells (http://www.punkhart.com/dylan/tapes/66-tour.html), and the EDLIS, BDBDB, (who has which boot database). I must point out that this site in no way sells bootlegs or even condones their sale. It is an archival site only:

Biograph (Official album - various tracks)

Masterpieces (Official album - 'Tom Thumb's Blues' from Liverpool)

So, after the official releases here is what we are left with -

A Week In The Life Bob Dylan And The Hawks 12 May - 17 May 1966, Gold Standard RAZ 014 CD (T- 392) (P)

Adelphi Theatre, Dublin, May 5th, 1966 Bob Dylan - Bulldog BGCD 008 CD (T - 119) (P).

Before The Crash, Vol 1 Bob Dylan (27 May 1966), Music With Love 003 CD (T - 235) (P).

Before The Crash; Vol 2 Bob Dylan & The Hawks (17 May 1966), Music With Love 003 CD (T - 235) (P).

Blowin' In The Wind Bob Dylan. (17 May 1966 - 31 Jan 74) CD (T - 361).

Bob Dylan Live Bob Dylan, (17 May 66) SW SW 70 CD (P).

Bob Dylan's Dream: Historic Live Performances Vol 1 Bob Dylan & The Band (19 April - 20 April 66), Living Legend LLRCD 005 CD (T - 118) (P).

Get Loud Bob Dylan. (10 May 66), Cuttlefish Records 013/014 3CD (T - 415) (Q).

Guitars Kissing & The Contemporary Fix Bob Dylan (17 May 66) Scorpio 51766A/E (orig) & SCO-8/9 (re) 2CD (T-024a) (Q).

Guitars Kissing & The Contemporary Fix Bob Dylan (Soundcheck version) (17 May 66) DPP Disc Hits 2CD (T-024b) (Q).

Hear The Document Bob Dylan (17 May 66) Blossom Music BD-17566 1/2 2CD.

Leicester '66 Bob Dylan & The Hawks (10 May 66 - 15 May 66) 2761-015 CD (T-299).

Like A Rolling Stone Bob Dylan & The Band (17 May 66) Vulture VT CD 006 (T-122) (P)

Live In England, May 66 Bob Dylan & The Band. (5 May - 17 May 66) Back Trax CD 04-88002 CD (T-124) (P).

Manchester Prayer Bob Dylan & The Hawks (17 May - 27 May 66) Swinging Pig TSP-CD-054 CD (T-120) (P).

Melbourne Bob Dylan & The Hawks (19 April - 20 April 66) Wanted Man Music WMM 023 CD (T-290) (P).

Melbourne, Australia/Bob Dylan & The Hawks (19 April 66) Wanted Man/Scorpio WMM 007/BD 93150 CD (T-236-237) (P).

Mr Tambourine Man. Vol 3 Bob Dylan (27 May 66) Apple House/Banana BAN-012-C CD (T-313) (P).

Pill Box Bob Dylan (20 May 66) TNT-940157/8 2CD (T-367) (P).

Play Fucking Loud Bob Dylan & The Hawks (14 May - 17 May 66) Supersound 93-BD-024 CD (T-266) (P).

Royal Albert Hall 1966 Bob Dylan & The Band (17 May 66) Swinging Pig TSP-CD-009 CD (T-121) (P).

Royal Albert Hall London May 26, 1966 Bob Dylan (17 May 66) Bulldog BGCD 001 CD (T-123) (P).

Sings The Body Electric Bob Dylan (14 May - 27 May 66) Parrot CD (T-041) (Q).

Spanish Is The Loving Tongue, Unplugged & Jamming Bob Dylan (1 May 66 - 20 Oct 94) Vol 2 CDR.

The Live Dylan With The Band Bob Dylan (5 May 66) Black Panther CD (T-279)

In 1970 the first vinyl boot of the wrongly named, *Bob Dylan-Royal Albert Hall* arrived. This is the record that led me on the long strange trip into writing this book. It featured the electric set only and went through many manifestations before turning up on CD, and finally being acknowledged as the Free Trade Hall.

What then followed on vinyl, CD and tape was a plethora of choices as to which gig, which recording, mono or stereo, audience or 'official', one wanted to go for. Partial recordings for Melbourne, Dublin, Sheffield, the Albert Hall and many other gigs survive. Those performances which appear to have been circulated on bootleg recordings are as follows -

Newport Festival, 25th July 1965 - An official line recording of Dylan's first electric set followed by 'Mr Tambourine Man' and 'It's All Over Now, Baby Blue.' This is available on CD and video. (Various titles)

Forest Hills, 28th August 1965 - Dylan's second outing with a backing band, this audience recording contains both acoustic and electric sets, plus howling and booing.

Chicago, 26th November 1965 - Another audience recording of four numbers from the second set - 'Tombstone Blues,' 'I Don't Believe You,' 'Baby Let me Follow You Down' and 'Ballad Of A Thin Man.'

Berkeley, 4th December 1965 - Dylan and The Hawks rocking on down on an audience recording notable for the inclusion of 'Long Distance Operator' and 'Positively 4th Street.'

All of the above are available on the ten CD Boxed Set, *Ten Of Hearts*.

White Plains, 5th February 1966 - A 57 minute long audience recording. Not of the best quality, but an interesting document.

Syria Mosque, 6th February 1966 - More poor quality audience tape featuring 6 acoustic and 2 electric, one of which is 'Positively 4th Street.'

Hempstead, 26th February 1966 - An audience recording. This is the set as it will be played throughout the World Tour.

Melbourne, 19th April 1966 - A proper stereo line recording of the acoustic section of the show, plus three electric numbers. The version of 'Just Like Tom Thumb's Blues' has the wonderful spoken introduction. Supposedly available as a CD, but I haven't come across one yet.

Dublin, 5th May 1966 - A PA tape of the first half. The inclusion of 'I Don't Believe You' on *Biograph* is tantalising. If they recorded that we have to assume that they recorded the entire set.

Bristol, 10th May 1966 - A poor quality audience tape of the gig is in existence.

Birmingham, 12th May 1966 - 'Ballad Of A Thin Man' taken from a line recording has appeared on bootleg CD *A Week In The Life*.

Liverpool, 14th May 1966 - Four tunes from the second set taken from official line recordings have appeared, one officially. The others are on *A Week In The Life*.

Leicester, 15th May 1966 - An partial audience recording has appeared on CD. (See above).

Sheffield, 16th May 1966 - Live recordings of 'Leopard Skin Pill-Box Hat' and 'One Too Many Mornings' have been released on the *A Week In The Life* CD.

Manchester, 17th May 1966 - One of the most bootlegged recordings ever made, the Free Trade Hall concert, acoustic and electric, has appeared as *Manchester Prayer, Guitars Kissing & The Contemporary Fix*, and recently with added tracks from elsewhere, a double CD entitled *Hear The Document*.

Edinburgh, 20th May 1966 - A couple of songs from the electric set have appeared on CD. An audience recording of the entire concert is available. (See above).

Royal Albert Hall, 26th May 1966 - Three acoustic and four electric tracks from Dylan's first night in London have appeared on bootlegs. (See above)

Royal Albert Hall, 27th May 1966 - The first half of the concert in its entirety has been released on bootleg under a variety of names. (See above).

There are rumours of a Stockholm audience tape, and, as this list is by no means supposed to be exhaustive, there are no doubt many others that people will be able to point out. Hopefully this is a reasonable guide to the material available out there. There are always rumours regarding the imminent release of the Free Trade Hall as an official Sony/Columbia project, but it keeps being continually put on the back burner. Who knows? One day they might just see the 'official' light of day.

APPENDIX THREE- Itinerary

1965

July 24, Newport Folk Festival
August 28, Forest Hills
September 3, Hollywood Bowl CA
September 24, Austin TX
September 25, Dallas TX
October 1, Carnegie Hall NY
October 2, Newark, NJ
October 9, Atlanta GA
October 15, Baltimore OH
October 16, Princeton NJ
October 17, Worcester MA
October 22, Providence RI
October 23, Burlington VT
October 24, Detroit MI
October 29, Boston MA
October 30, Hartford CT
October 31, Boston MA
November 4, Minneapolis MN
November 6, Buffalo NY
November 12, Cleveland OH
November 14 & 15, Toronto
November 18, Cincinnati OH
November 19, Columbus OH
November 20, Rochester NY
November 21, Syracuse NY
December 4, Berkeley CA
December 5 & 11, San Francisco CA
December 10, San Diego CA
December 12 San Jose CA
December 18, Pasadena CA
December 19, Santa Monica CA

1966

February 5, White Plains NY
February 6, Pittsburgh PA
February 7, Louisville KY
February 10, Memphis TN
February 11, Richmond VA
February 12, Norfolk VA
February 19, Ontario
February 20, Quebec
February 24 & 25, Philadelphia PA
February 26, Hempstead NY
March 3, Miami FL
March 11, St Louis MO
March 12, Lincoln NE
March 13, Denver CO
March 24, Portland OR
March 25, Seattle WA
March 26, Vancouver
March 27, Tacoma WA
April 9, Honolulu
April 13, Sydney
April 15, Brisbane
April 16, Sydney
April 19 & 20, Melbourne
April 22, Adelaide
April 23, Perth
April 29, Stockholm
May 1, Copenhagen
May 5, Dublin
May 10, Bristol
May 11, Cardiff
May 12, Birmingham
May 14, Liverpool
May 15, Leicester
May 16, Sheffield
May 17, Manchester
May 19, Glasgow
May 20, Edinburgh
May 21, Newcastle
May 24, Paris
May 26 & 27, London
July 29th 1966 - Motorbike crash.

APPENDIX FOUR
Internet Resources

The best way to start searching on the Web for Dylan related sites is to go to the *Bringing It All Back Homepage* (see below). Surprisingly, and I don't know why I say that, Sony/Columbia also offer an extremely good Dylan site run by Dan Levy (see below). This Web page has a variety of audio/visual treats which change from week to week. At the time of writing you could download audio clips that are hitherto unavailable on official release, plus video extracts. Highly recommended.

At this point words must be said about *EDLIS* (Electronic Dylan Lyric Information Service). They are a highly motivated unofficial group of devotees who spend much of their time on the Web sorting out databases of information regarding gigs, gatherings, and archival material.

Bob Dylan on the World Wide Web

A Web page is a means of providing user friendly access to information, in the form of text, pictures, sounds and animations via the Internet. It can draw upon resources from around the world to present about a given topic. Consider, for example, a web page which aims to cover the 1996 Bob Dylan tour. At a few clicks of a button, you would expect to be able to access from this page all the date and venue information, setlists, statistics, the band's cue sheets, photographs and first-hand reviews.

For more detailed information about the Web and how to access it, refer to your Internet provider, software manuals and computer magazines. The best recommendation, though, is to impose on a knowledgeable friend for a few hours.

Bob Dylan content on the Web has grown enormously since the first page appeared in 1994 courtesy of John Howells. The trend in recent years has been towards greater specialisation, and therefore greater depth of knowledge and information, so as to avoid continual re-inventing of the wheel.

Below you will find a brief guide to some of the quality Bob Dylan Web pages, a mere taste of what is currently available.

The Web is by nature evolutionary, such that daily updated pages are common place. While usually a blessing, this fluidity makes the fixed list below necessarily out of date from the moment it has finished being compiled. Web page locations, names and content may well have altered by the time you read this. Some may even have ceased to exist.

However, help is at hand because it is common for Web pages covering similar topics to be linked to each other. If you can find one of the Web pages listed below, chances are you will find the others. At worst, one can venture over to one of the mighty Search Engines (which attempt to index all known pages world-wide) and try a few obvious key words.

Here are a list of Dylan related Internet addresses which the reader may find of interest, compiled by Ben Taylor.

VARIOUS CONTENT

Boblinks (Bill Pagel)

Links to most Bob Dylan pages on the Internet.

http://www.execpc.com/~billp61/boblink.html

Breadcrumb Sins (Giulio Molfese)

Includes interviews, photographs, articles and original artwork.

http://www.interferenza.com/bcs/

Bringing It All Back Home (John Howells)

Includes tape reviews, general news and articles.

http://www.punkhart.com/dylan/index.html

EDLIS

Includes archive of common discussion topics.

http://www.edlis.org/

Expecting Rain (Karl Erik Anderson)

Includes general news, original art gallery, tour reviews and pictures.

http://www.expectingrain.com/

Official Bob Dylan web page

Includes lyrics, articles and otherwise unavailable sound recordings.

http://www.bobdylan.com

TOUR INFORMATION

Boblinks Tour Page (Bill Pagel)

The primary source of up to date tour information, including well-informed rumours.

http://www.execpc.com/~billp61/dates.html

Olof Bjorner's yearly summaries

Detailed setlist information from 1960 onwards.

http://reality.sgi.com/employees/howells/olof.html

RELIGION

Bob Dylan: Tangled Up In Jews (Larry Yudelson)

The Jewish religious and cultural odyssey of Bob Dylan.

http://www.well.com/user/yudel/dylan.html

Slow Train Coming (Bill Parr)

The impact of Christianity on Bob Dylan's work and life.

http://funnelweb.utcc.utk.edu/~wparr/SlowTrain.html

FANZINES

Inside A Prune (Andrew Muir). Homer The Slut magazine

http://www.zimmy.demon.co.uk/contents.htm

Isis Magazine

http://www.interferenza.com/bcs/isis.htm

COVER SONGS

Cowboy Angel Sings (Andra Greenberg)

Songs covered by Bob Dylan: includes background information,performance dates and links to lyrics: http://cvrc.med.upenn.edu/~greenberg/

Recordings of Bob Dylan by other artists (Olof Bjorner and Steve Farowich):

ftp://ftp.neda.com/pub/dylan/olof/covers/by-song.html

INFLUENCES

Routes & Ramblings (Manfred Helfert):

http://www.yi.com/home/HelfertManfred/

Roots Of Bob (Seth Kulick). Examination of influences for specific songs.

http://www.cis.upenn.edu/~skulick/edlis.html

DISCUSSION GROUPS

HWY61-L mailing list (MaureenLeblanc):

http://home.earthlink.net/~hporter/index.html.Rec.music.dylan newsgroup

Frequently Asked Questions (John Howells)

http://www.punkhart.com/dylan/faq.html

TIME CAPSULES

Blonde On Blonde: Bob Dylan in Melbourne, 1966 (Tricia Jungwirth)

http://www.geocities.com/Heartland/Hills/5581/

Bob Dylan: His Life and Work, 1964-1966 (William D. Glenn)

http://www.ddg.com/LIS/glenn/DYLANWEB.HTM

REGIONAL

Grains of Sand (Andreas Gustaffson) Sweden http://www.gson.com/gos/

German Affairs (Christian Zeiser) http://www.yi.com/home/ZeiserChristian/

Italian Affairs (Giulio Molfese) http://www.interferenza.com/bcs/bd_italy.htm

BIBLIOGRAPHY

Dylan Bibliography (Ron Chester)

An extremely detailed catalogue of Dylan-related books

http://www.taxhelp.com/

APPENDIX FIVE
Some Thoughts On The Month Of May

As the researches for this book rolled along I began to notice a recurrent theme - the month of May.

Dylan first came to Manchester in May (1964). He returned almost exactly a year later in 1965, and then again for the (in)famous Free Trade Hall gig almost exactly a year after that. It strikes me as somewhat of a coincidence that every year at around the same time a particular person is geographically placed within a specific space, given the fact that a performer's life is supposedly driven by chance. Then I also realised it was Dylan's birthday on the 24th May, so I began to look at other events relating to both May and Bob Dylan.

For what it's worth, here are some interesting snipppets: not all of them meant to be taken entirely seriously.

May is known for the goddess Maia, who was the mother of Mercury. Does 'thin, wild, mercury music' ring any bells? In alchemical terms Mercury has several meanings - Quicksilver, of course, being the most readily identifiable - but it also pertains to the universal aspect of a substance, its 'spirit' let's say, as distinguished from its universal character. So in animal alchemy, Mercury represents consciousness.

In mythology, Mercury was the messenger of the gods and wore a winged cap and winged shoes to speed his flight (Maggie comes fleet foot). He always carried a rod entwined with two serpents. Most important of all, however, is that Mercury is said to have invented the lyre, and is therefore the inventor of all stringed instruments. Seems he hollowed out a tortoise shell one day and strung nine cords of linen across it representing the nine muses. With this he made music that delighted the gods.

So Mercury, the son of Maia, became a symbol of universal consciousness, master of language and creator of music.

May Day (May 1st) is celebrated all around the world as a worker's holiday, but its origins as a festival go back thousands of years particularly in the northern hemisphere where it represented the return of light (summer) after the darkness of winter. In Celtic culture it's called Beltane and is observed by the lighting of bonfires. On May morning people would find their doors garlanded with flowers. Trees lopped of their branches and wrapped around with coloured cloths were erected on village greens, Maypoles, as they are known. Shakespeare said that people could hardly sleep on May Eve they were so excited. Maidens would rise before dawn to wash their faces in the 'May dew', forever to keep their young looks. The festivities could last for days at a time.

Obviously music is closely associated with these festivals and the songs that celebrate May are almost too numerous to mention, but in relation to Bob Dylan, synchronicity, life, the universe and everything, here are two interesting samples.

On May 8th, the feast of the apparition of St Michael the Archangel, the girls of Helston in Cornwall are dressed in white linen gowns and bedecked with garlands of flowers and leaves. They dance widdershins (anti-clockwise) around the town accompanied by their 'guardians', young men dressed in green. The tune that they dance to is the original 'Lord Of The Dance' as popularised by the very Sidney Carter who was the host of the 'Hallelujah' TV show Dylan appeared in 1964.

Another 'May tune' that is worthy of consideration is called 'As I Walked Out,' and was popularised by the singing Copper family of Rottingdean in Sussex. The Coppers had been singing in their local area for generations and much of their repertoire is impossible to date. 'As I Walked Out' is at least two hundred years old. Dylan would certainly have been aware of the Copper Family who had been 'discovered' by the English folk scene in the 1950s, and who had recorded several albums for Bill Leader's label.

But why should this song be of particular significance? It's a straightforward ballad of unrequited love. The singer, stepping out on a May morning, comes across a beautiful Irish girl -

'So red and rosy were her cheeks and coal black was her hair

And costly was the robe of gold this Irish girl did wear.'

The young man falls in love with her, but her heart is with another. He dreams of how he can get close to her...

'I wish I was a butterfly, I'd fly to my love's breast,

And if I were a linnet I would sing my love to rest,'

But the most interesting line to Dylan afficianados of this ageless love song comes at the top of the second verse when the singer describes the Irish girl -

'Her shoes were made of Spanish leather all sprinkled o'er with dew...'

Here we've got a combination of pagan May ritual combined with an idea that Dylan would later adopt in his own song, 'Boots Of Spanish Leather'.

Coincidences and influences, all part of the magic of May...

ACKNOWLEDGMENTS

This is a book that probably took 32 years to write. In which case the cast of people who manouvered me into this position is far to long to list. However, with all due respect to the folks over the years who've encouraged me to keep on writing about this, that, and the other, here are the people I'd like to thank for their kindness, encouragement and friendship whilst getting *Like The Night* together.

In no particular order, but pedantically trying to keep it at the very least chronological, the whole exercise was inaugerated by my PhD supervisor, Dr Steve Redhead, who rather liked the chapter I did on Bob Dylan in Manchester for my thesis. Many thanks to Any Spinoza at *The Manchester Evening News*, and Chris Sharratt of *City Life*, who thrust the project forward. From that, and other weird things, I was able to meet, via the Internet, and then in the flesh, a group of people who have sustained, nourished and nurtured this project through until its completion. Before naming them I have to say that anybody who spends a little time on the rec.music.dylan newsgroup, or who trawls through the voluminous archives of EDLIS, or Highway 61 Listserve, will find a lively, intelligent group of netizens devoted to studying the life and works of Bob Dylan. It's a rewarding experience to come across them in cyberspace (more so in the flesh). The work that they carry out is both informative and entertaining.

That said, without the stalwart assistance of Ben Taylor (who compiled the Internet resources section for this book), Craig Jamieson and Alan Fraser, it's hard to imagine this volume having been completed. They have assisted, enabled and informed, sometimes at considerable expense to themselves, but, gee, aw shucks guys, ain't that why you're there?

Also in the murky depths of cyberspace I have been able to come into contact with enthusiasts like Larry Horton in New York, to whom, much thanks, and John Howells, both of whom have helped this project in their own unique ways.

Before bidding a fond farewell to the Internet, I have to say how useful it has been in relation to being able to make contacts with people that it may otherwise have taken weeks/months to establish. In particular I want to thank Tricia Jungwirth in Australia, not only for offering me comments on the work in progress, but also for providing me with information and artefacts relating to Bob Dylan and the world tour that have proved invaluable in the writing of this book (see Appendix for Tricia's own Dylan 66 Web site).

Meanwhile, back on Planet Earth, the next stage in the genesis of this particular volume occurred when *Mojo* Magazine in the form of Bleddyn Butcher approached me for my comments on the Free Trade hall gig, and lo and behold, an article appeared. Thus fired by an enthusiasm that bordered on, well, enthusiasm, I started researching the book.

The first thing to happen was what we in the North call, 'down the pub', where Steve Currie, who was there that fateful night, suggested that I contact a guy who'd also been present, and had taken a load of photos. Thus began my relationship with Paul Kelly, who, as I write, resides in the Hindu Kush, but I'm sure would like me to extend his thanks to Gill, his wife and his son Adam, who await his imminent return.

A great bunch of friends then began their 'support group' activities. These were people who were as interested as I was in Dylan's 1966 tour and wanted to see what the research would unveil. Some of them were there, some weren't, but what the heck?

It is unto them that I am eternally indebted for their help, assistance and other things, over and above the call of duty. Most of all, Richard Boon who kept the flame burning when I was at my lowest. Richard Thomas and Howard Devoto, your names are called with pride. In Manchester, Bob and Caroline Dickinson, and Jim Aulich. In London, Mat Snow at *Mojo*. At the time domiciled in, but never sent to, Coventry, Derek Barker at *Isis* Magazine.

Over in San Francisco, Greil Marcus read several variants of the manuscript and was only too happy to help with suggestions and revisions. For an author of his stature to be involved with a first time project by an unknown author says more about his character than it does about my writing. Thank you Greil, you have been my grail.

Next, I have to take time out to thank Bob Dylan's publisher, Jeff Rosen of Dwarf Music, for all the time and attention that he's paid to the project. Jeff has dealt swiftly and reasonably with all the requests that I've made upon his time. Once again, thanks.

And now, the people without whom this book really would not have been possible - those of us who were there that night all those years ago, and, those who were there in spirit.

Many thanks for giving me your time, your memories, and your opinions -

Once again, in no particular order -

Roger and Jane Harvey, Bob Jones, Dave Stott, Mike King, Ken Birch, Rick Saunders, Barbara Murray, Doreen McGhee, Dave Rothwell, Steve Curie, Rick Saunders, Tim Green and Kath Green, Kevin Fletcher, Stewart Trey, Malcolm Metcalfe, Neville Kellett, Dave Stott, Pete Dawson, Peter Barnes, Joe Boyd, D.A. Pennebaker, Bob Harding, and Chris Clover. Walter from The Dolly Tub Laundrette. Lonnie 'X' and all the guys at the Politburo.

My thanks would be incomplete if I didn't include my colleagues at the Department of Media and Performance at the University of Salford who valiantly put up with my strange behaviour and occasional whoops of delight as 'exotic' and 'rare' tapes arrived in my pigeonhole.

So, thanks to Anna Vowles, Gareth Palmer and Head of Department, Ron Cook.

Paul Kelly, the erstwhile 15 year old wunderkind of photo-verite lent his more than ample hand to the completion of this document. Car journeys to interviews, suggestions as regards the manuscript, encouragement when it was most needed. Thanks Paul, whose negatives were ripped off many years ago, but whose pictures have appeared on countless bootleg covers and magazines ever since. I trust we've set the record straight once and for all, and that you, the reader, like what you see.

A small but select group of publishers were presented with the outline for this book. Not one of them were interested until I came across Sean Body and Helter Skelter. Call them insane, or, call them inspired. Sean and the rest of the crew at the store had the imagination and the foresight to go ahead with what they thought was a worthwhile project. Sean has proven to be not only a good editor, but a great publisher.

Finally - it's a cliché, I know. But in this instance it's true. To the woman without whom all this would have been impossible - I refer, of course, to my wife Pam. She really is the poor sod who sits there while I moan, whine, whinge, and generally go on. Until, that is, that fateful day when I ask, 'Would you like to sort all this out for me?'

She does it, and with a love that's so fine it nearly blows my mind.

Need I say more?

Thank you.

Index

Available Now From Helter Skelter Publishing

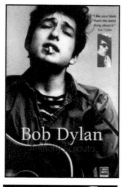

Bob Dylan by Anthony Scaduto 1-900924-00-5 £11.95
The first and best biography of Dylan.

"Scaduto's 1971 book was the pioneering portrait of this legendarily elusive artist. Now in a welcome reprint it's a real treat to read the still-classic Bobography".
Paul Du Noyer, Q***

"Superb on the Greenwich Village scene, insightful on the meaning of John Wesley Harding ... it's still perhaps the best book ever written on Dylan".
Peter Doggett, *Record Collector*

A Journey Through America With The Rolling Stones by Robert Greenfield   1-900924-01-3 £12.00
Definitive insider's account of the Stones' legendary 1972 US tour.

"Greenfield is afforded extraordinary access to the band... drugs... groupies. In all, it's a graphic if headache inducing document of strange days indeed".
Tom Doyle, Q***

"Sure, I was completely mad. I go crazy."
Mick Jagger

Back To The Beach - A Brian Wilson and the Beach Boys Reader edited by Kingley Abbott 1-900924-02-1 £12.99

Featuring a foreword by Brian Wilson, Back to the Beach is a collection of the best articles about the band, including a number of pieces specially commissioned for this volume.

"Pet Sounds was my inspiration for making Sgt Pepper." **Paul McCartney**

Coming Soon From Helter Skelter publishing:

Born In The USA - Bruce Springsteen and the American Tradition by Jim Cullen 1-900924-05-6 £9.99

The first major study of Bruce Springsteen's that looks at his music in the context of his blue collar roots, and his place in American culture

"This is a provocative look at one of America's cultural icons." **Newsweek**

Available From Firefly Publishing

an association between Helter Skelter and SAF Publishing

**Poison Heart - Surviving The Ramones by Dee Dee Ramone
and Veronica Kofman   ISBN: 0946 719 19 5
192 pages (illustrated). UK £11.95**
A crushingly honest account of his life as a junkie and a Ramone.
"One of THE great rock and roll books...this is the true, awesome voice of The Ramones". **Q magazine** *****
"His story - knee deep in sex, drugs and rock and roll - is too incident packed to be anything less than gripping". **Mojo**
"A powerful work that is both confessional and exorcising" **Time Out.**

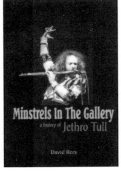

**Minstrels In The Gallery - A History of Jethro Tull by David Rees
ISBN: 0 946719 22 5   224 pages (illustrated) - UK £12.99**
At Last! To coincide with their 30th anniversary, a full history of one of the most popular and inventive bands of the past three decades. Born out of the British blues boom, Jethro Tull sped to almost worldwide success and superstardom. Fronted by the wild showmanship of Ian Anderson, the band were one of the biggest grossing acts of the seventies. With LPs like *Aqualung,Thick As A Brick* and *Passion Play*, Anderson mutated from the wild-eyed tramp through flute wielding minstrel to the country squire of rock n' roll. David Rees is *the* foremost authority on Jethro Tull - he has interviewed all the band members for this intriguing book.

**DANCEMUSICSEXROMANCE - Prince: The First Decade
by Per Nilsen   ISBN: 0946 719 23 3
200 pages approx (illustrated). UK £tbc**
For many years Per Nilsen has been a foremost authority on Prince. In this in-depth study of the man and his music, he assesses the years prior to the change of name to a symbol - a period which many consider to be the most productive and musically satisfying. Through interview material with many ex-band members and friends Nilsen paints a portrait of Prince's reign as the most exciting black performer to emerge since James Brown. In this behind the scenes documentary we get to the heart and soul of a funk maestro.

All Helter Skelter and Firefly titles can be ordered direct from the world famous Helter Skelter music bookstore which is situated at:

Helter Skelter,
4 Denmark Street, London WC2H 8LL
Tel: +44 (0) 171 836 1151   Fax: +44 (0) 171 240 9880.
Consult our website at: http://www.skelter.demon.co.uk

This store has the largest collection of music books anywhere in the world and can supply any in-print title by mail to any part of the globe. For a mail order catalogue or for wholesaling enquiries, please contact us.